HYMNS AND PSALMS,

OR

Songs of Prayer and Praise

TO

ALMIGHTY GOD.

BY S. J. HOLBROOK.

Clothed in love with power supreme,
The mighty Saviour did appear;
Salvation was his only theme,
His great and glorious mission here.

That love that moved the Father's breast
To send the mighty Saviour down,
That love so pure his Son possessed,
He wrought for man a richer crown.

NORTH WRENTHAM:
1854.

PREFACE.

The Author of this little work, before introducing it to the public, would like to make a few remarks by way of apology, as he does not pretend to be a book-maker or a poet; but being in feeble health, unable to labor, has given him time for thought and reflection; he has therefore composed this little book. He would further remark, through the whole of it he has tried to let party spirit or sectarianism entirely alone—to judge not lest he be judged. Leave that to God, who searches the heart and trieth the reins.

Four things, oh God, pray let me learn,
Before my lamp shall cease to burn;
Thy Love, thy Mercy and thy Grace,
The Path to Heaven, thy dwelling place.

And thus while in this lonely vale,
While life and strength begin to fail,
Yet while this throbbing heart shall beat,
Prepare, my soul, My God to meet.

CONTENTS.

HYMNS.

A

B

Hymn.

E

F

G

H

Hymn.

I

J

L

Hymn.

M

N

O

P

R

S

T

V

W

Y

PSALMS.

B

C

R

T

W

Hymns and Spiritual Songs.

HYMN 1.

A View of God's Power and Goodness.

While alone I sit and ponder
   On our Creator's vast domain,
My feeble thoughts from earth do wander,
   Such heavenly views I can't contain.

While viewing God, the sole Creator,
   Who formed the earth and made the skies,
Created light to cheer all nature,
   The moon and stars He made likewise.

It's oft I am lost in meditation,
   Oft I exclaim with great surprise,
That He who rules this great creation
   Lives eternal in the skies.

I view Him there in all His glory,
 Then of creating power I think,
Wonders rise like clouds before me,
 Oh, into nothing then I shrink.

A gleam of hope is still arising,
 That powerful God doth care for me;
His love to man, oh! how surprising—
 His face in Heaven I hope to see.

There to dwell with Him in glory,
 From sin's alluring charms set free;
There tell the Saints the pleasing story,
 How Christ who died remembered me.

To hear the Saints and Angels singing,
 Holy is the God of host;
The heavenly courts with praises ringing
 To Father, Son and Holy Ghost.

HYMN 2.

A View of God's Tender Mercies.

When I recount Thy mercies o'er,
And think how negligent we are,
I fain would wish to sin no more,
Or trample on Thy tender care.

I pray that hence I may be wise—
Choose the good part that Mary did;
My daily life the world surprise,
My concience every sin forbid.

May I be found a righteous man,
No sin my heart or conscience stain;
On earth do all the good I can,
At last a crown of glory gain.

Then when I die may I remove
To that bright Heaven beyond the skies,
Rejoicing in a Saviour's love,
And that great God so just and wise.

There may I sit at His right hand,
  Rejoicing in that Heaven above;
Fulfilled by faith that great command,
  That all His Saints I once had loved.

Oh, then my joys will be complete,
  God will my happiness control;
I'll sit and sing at Jesus's feet
  The wonders of my ransomed soul.

HYMN 3.

Agur's Prayer.—Pr. 30, 8.

In Agur's prayer he wished to be
  From poverty and wealth set free;
I think his reason must be this—
  No wealth I want but heavenly bliss.

May that my happy portion be,
  Was Agur's prayer, it seems to me;
Just what I want in ample store,
  May I not wish or covet more.

For what I want from day to day,
  Oh, may Thy servant Agur pray;
And for that prize to mortals given
  A place with Thee, my God, in Heaven.

HYMN 4.

A View of the Nature of Sin.

When I survey my former life,
  And think how negligent I live;
Engaged in folly, sin and strife,
  I think how can my God forgive.

I hope by faith and humble prayer,
  And strict obedience to His word,
To wash away the stains I wear,
  And hold communion with the Lord.

But Satan, with malicious art,
  Tries to lead my feet astray;
He watches each unguarded heart,
  And tells them Christ is not the way.

When I survey that dreadful tree,
  And see where Christ my Saviour died ;
He suffered this for you and me—
  A natural death He was denied.

HYMN 5.

Meditation on the Crucifixion.

The Saviour's love so great we see
  That on the cross for man He died ;
He suffered shame on Calvary,
  And cruel soldiers pierced His side.

On His head they placed a crown of thorns,
  Gave Him gall and vinegar to drink ;
Reviled with mockery and scorn—
  Such wondrous love, what can we think !

Three hours in anguish on the tree
  The purple gore gushed from His side ;
This to atone for you and me,
  Then bowed His lovely head and died.

Then darkness o'er the land was spread,
The temple vail was rent in twain;
The Jews they mocked and wagged their heads
When Christ the lamb of God was slain.

While on the Cross the Saviour cried,
The earth it quaked, the rocks were rent;
Behold My hands, My feet and side,
Then, oh! vile man, thou must repent.

Repent, I say, and thou shalt live
In Paradise above with me;
Oh, pray in faith, God will forgive,
Then Christ in glory thou shalt see.

HYMN 6.

God's high abode, that righteous place,
Beyond the blue ethereal skies;
There He has built a throne of grace,
Made that heart-rending sacrifice.

He sacrificed our great High Priest,
  Who tasted death, then rose again;
He spread that grand, that living feast,
  Before the fallen race of man.

That living feast of living bread,
  The soul that eats shall never die;
Christ did His work, then kindly said,
  Prepare to meet me in the sky.

Prepare to meet thy final doom,
  To meet with joy, and not with grief;
There have thy wedding garments on,
  Then thou shalt find God's kind relief.

His kind relief, so freely given,
  To those who pray with fervent faith;
The meek, the lowly, dwell in Heaven,
  Thus the great Redeemer saith.

There make those Heavenly regions ring
  With music from the golden lyre;
Far sweeter than the tints of Spring,
  To Heaven our nobler thoughts aspire.

HYMN 7.

A View of God's Infinite Power and Tender Care.

When I survey the heavens above,
 And think of worlds beyond the skies,
I ponder on a Saviour's love—
 A gracious God, so just and wise.

I fear lest I in woe be lost,
 Or pass unnoticed by his care ;
With all the blessed on Canaan's coast,
 May I be found amongst them there.

But when I think of worlds unknown,
 As numerous as the stars you see,
I think how God from his bright throne,
 Doth care for souls as small as me.

So I'll have faith in his dear Son,
 And pray my sins may be forgiven ;
May I that race of glory run,
 And be admitted into heaven.

There I shall see that great first cause,
  Of all in heaven and all on earth;
And wonder why that powerful God
  Should care for me since I had birth.

HYMN 8.

On Zion's glittering mount there stands
  A place sublime to pilgrims given;
God's holy house not made with hands,
  There is eternal in the heavens.

God's house of rest where glory reigns,
  There the Saints and Angels dwell,
And shout and sing in sweetest strains,
  Christ Jesus has done all things well.

That heavenly host, there cherubims
  Join the soft, the golden lays;
The new Millennium day begins
  With souls whom God sees fit to raise.

Now when on Pisgah's top we stand,
  Our thoughts ascend within the vale;
There view by faith the promised land,
  Then trust in Christ, we cannot fail.

HYMN 9.

A Good Resolution.

When I resolve to do his will,
  And keep my conscience clear,
His precepts daily to fulfil,
  I find a Saviour near.

But when my faith and love grow cold,
  Absorbed in earthly care,
The tempter then grows strong and bold,
  I lose my strength in prayer.

But when with faith and love I pray
  To that great God in heaven,
He will banish all my fears away,
  And speak my sins forgiven.

Thus while I live I wish to be
  In truth as good as I profess,
From sin's alluring charms set free,
  A Saviour's love possess.

Then when my race is run below,
  And time is no more with me,
May I from thence to glory go—
  God's smiling face to see.

There may I wear a starry crown,
  And walk those streets of gold ;
With Saints and Angels there sit down,
  Those wonders to behold.

There to hear those harps of gold
  Sound sweetly o'er the heavenly plains ;
The Saints whose bliss cannot be told,
  While glory, glory is their strains.

There to dwell in worlds above,
  And strike those golden harps of praise ;
To shout and sing redeeming love
  At God's right hand through endless days.

HYMN 10.

To thee, Great God! we make our moan,
  Who holds the keys of life and death;
We supplicate Thy righteous throne ;
  May we repent while we have breath.

Before that awful day shall come,
  When we must stand before Thy face,
There to hear our final doom,
  O, save us with Thy sovereign grace!

Lord! we approach Thee through Thy Son,
  And call upon Thy sacred name ;
Teach us to say, " Thy will be done!"
  Throughout this earthly frame.

Lord of Mercy! hear our prayer,
  With pity view our wretched case;
Permit our feet to enter there,
  And worship round Thy throne of grace!

HYMN 11.

Meditation on the Value of Time.

I asked a man whose hoary head
  Bespoke the ravages of time:
Time, Time, the golden hour, he said,
  The path to happiness sublime.

I asked a man at middle age,
  Whom grief had furrowed more than years:
Time, Time is to man life's busy stage,
  The guardian hope of all our fears.

I asked a youth whose blooming cheek,
  Promised health and length of days;
How false the joys such looks bespeak,
  For time destroys in divers ways.

I asked myself, Oh, what is time?
  Just like a bubble on the wave,
It steals away this life of mine,
  And brings the cold, the silent grave.

Old Father Time, I asked his haste :
  His answer quick and stern he gave,
"Young man, there is no time to waste !"
  Then on he rushed toward the grave.

Next asked the holy Angel, who shall stand,
  To sound the trump, God's hidden mysteries
One foot on sea, and one on land, [o'er,
  Time was, and is; but time shall be no more.

HYMN 12.

Christ the Lord from glory came,
  Hosanna to his sacred name,
He tasted death that we might live,
  He will the contrite soul forgive.

Then whilst my lamp holds out to burn,
  May I from sin and vice return,
And thus defend my Maker's cause,
  And read His word and mind His laws.

Now while I dwell, a Pilgrim here,
  Teach me Thy love, Thy wrath to fear,
Protect the brittle thread of life,
  Keep me from hatred, sin and strife.

HYMN 13.

Behold, our loving Saviour bled,
  High on the cross He died for me,
Without a crime His blood was shed,
  With rugged nails, nailed to the tree.

While on the cross He paid the debt,
  'T was there the Jews His blood they spilt,
He prayed till drops of blood He sweat,
  And died to save us from our guilt.

HYMN 14.

God's Love to Man.

Great God of all, in Heaven and Earth,
  Who made my soul for realms of bliss,
Eternal life and solid mirth,
  May I not lose a prize like this.

I must not waste this precious time,
  But make my peace with God above,
That happy place will then be mine,
  To shout and sing redeeming love.

Thy love to man, poor feeble man,
  Whom Thou hast made, thine image given
His days and years seem but a span,
  Just time to trace his path to heaven.

Now while I have probation given,
  I must not waste that precious hour,
I'll pray to God who dwells in heaven,
  That He would shield me with his power.

Oh, may Thy love my heart entwine,
  Salvation be my greatest aim,
Thy saving grace, that gem, be mine,
  While I a Saviour's love proclaim.

Ah, what is man, 'tis plain to see,
  Compared with Thy eternal might,
From vice and sin he must be free,
  Then Christ will save his heart's delight.

Thy love to all the human race,
  Who reap the fruits of Adam's fall,
Oh, may I see thy smiling face,
  While on thy love depends my all.

HYMN 15.

A Dismissal.

Great God! dismiss us in thy fear,
  Teach us to know thy love and truth,
To ponder well on what we hear
  From hoary heads to giddy youth.

Teach us, oh Lord, thy holy will,
To believe and worship day by day,
Thy laws and precepts to fulfil,
And learn to watch as well as pray.

HYMN 16.

A Saviour's Love to Sinful Man.

A man of sin was heard to say:
Sad is my fate if I should die
While travelling in this sinful way,
For safety then, where shall I fly.

The Saviour heard his mournful voice,
With love and pity, lo! he cried,
Repent and live, with me rejoice,
To save thy soul I once have died.

These tender words in tones so sweet,
Caused this vile man to see his case;
He fell prostrate at Jesus's feet,—
Oh, there he found a hiding place.

There on his face for mercy cried,
  God heard and spoke his sins forgiven:
"My Son for thee was crucified,
  To save thy soul with him in heaven.

Arise! stand up! and still rejoice,
  Thy sins I freely all forgive."
Oh, then he heard that lovely voice,
  Through faith in me thy soul shall live.

Oh, may my heart that love possess:
  This man of sin in Jesus found
A place in Heaven—that glorious rest—
  While he lay prostrate on the ground.

Great God, wilt thou my portion be,
  Direct my feet in wisdom's ways;
May I thy realms of glory see,
  And sing thy praise through endless days.

HYMN 17.

The Star of Bethlehem.

In the city of David our Saviour was born,
And laid in a manger, his case looked forlorn;
He was born in that city, a distance afar,
Was known by the name of the Bethlehem star.

Now Joseph and Mary at Cæsar's request,
Their taxes to pay was a Bethlehem guest,
Although Mary had come from a distance afar,
Gave birth to a son, the Bethlehem star.

There Shepherds around were guarding their sheep,
In the land of Judea their flocks they did keep,
When an angel in glory appeared from afar,
And brought the good news of the Bethlehem star.

In the land of Judea they told the good news,
To the nations all round, as well as the Jews :
To see the young babe they came from afar,
To know the whole truth of the Bethlehem star.

The Shepherds believed, the glad tidings made known,
The holy child Jesus were joyous to own,
And wise men had heard, and they came from afar,
To worship the Saviour, the Bethlehem star.

The news of the Saviour was scattered abroad,
While thousands believed in the birth of their Lord ;
Then Simeon came, and men from afar,
To see the Lord Christ, the Bethlehem star.

HYMN 18.

Faith and Repentance.

Repent, vile man! the Saviour cried
  Have faith in me, and be forgiven;
Forsake thy sins and foolish pride,
  And make thy peace with God in heaven.

Repent, believe, and be baptized,
  And choose the robe that Angels wear,
For I, myself, was sacrificed
  To gain thy soul admittance there.

Go preach my gospel through the land,
  Remission given through faith in me;
Repentance is my great command,
  God's saving grace to all is free.

Faith and repentance work by love,
  To purify from sin and shame,
Direct man's thoughts to heaven above,
  To love and praise God's holy name.

Repent through faith, be justified,
And lay thy carnal weapons down ;
Behold thy Saviour crucified,
To gain for thee a starry crown.

Oh, may my heart with love and fear,
Confess my sins and be forgiven,
And try to keep my conscience clear,
To win that prize to mortals given.

Thy holy love my heart inspire,
God's glory be my only aim;
To do thy will, my fond desire,
A Saviour's dying love proclaim.

HYMN 19.

Great God, may we not be denied,
Show us the way and guard our feet;
The way the holy prophets tried,
That leads us to thy mercy seat.

Thy throne of mercy, far on high,
There Angels bow before thy face,
To do thy will I mean to try,
And trust the riches of thy grace.

We should almost forsake our clay,
Could we but claim them as our own,
Christ calls and saith I am the way,
I'll pray to thee through him alone.

Ah! woe is me should I refuse,
Despise the path my Saviour trod,
And like the unbelieving Jews,
Call down the vengeance of our God.

HYMN 20.

I would possess that love unfeigned,
Pure, undefiled before the Lord;
Through faith that blessing is obtained—
By prayer, and trusting in his word.

That love that moved our Saviour's God,
  To bring salvation from above;
The path of blood and death he trod,
  Constrained by pity and by love.

Our Maker, God of love and grace,
  Prepared that soul-reviving feast;
The Saviour here unveiled his face,
  Our advocate, our great High Priest.

HYMN 21.

Great are the Heavens, but greater still
  Is our Creator's holy will;
He rules the whole with powerful sway,
  He turns the darkness into day.

The darkness flies before his voice,
  His light makes heaven and earth rejoice;
Let there be light, Jehovah said,
  Then light appeared and darkness fled.

John the Gospel's light did preach,
  In dreary wilds the word did teach ;
He preached of Christ, the great Messiah
  Who was foretold by Jeremiah.

This light the old Apostles tried,
  They took the Saviour for their guide;
The patriarchs and prophets too,
  Kept their Saviour's path in view.

HYMN 22.

God's Promise Endureth Forever.

Firm as a rock thy promise stands,
  The saving grace and mercies free,
Teach me to keep thy great commands
  With faith in Christ and love to thee.

Eternal wisdom has ordained
  A plan through Christ, our souls to save,
And shown how this can be obtained,
  That bliss secured beyond the grave.

I must not then so slothful be,
   But try to gain that golden prize;
Thy dazzling throne, oh, may I see
   In regions pure beyond the skies.

There I would rest my weary soul,
   From sorrow, pain, and sin set free,
To sing thy praise while ages roll,
   And all those heavenly beauties see.

I would secure that glorious bliss,
   To dwell with all the saints in heaven;
How can I lose a prize like this?
   I'll pray through faith to be forgiven.

Grant me thy counsel for my guide,
   Direct my feet in wisdom's ways;
Forgive my sins and haughty pride,
   Teach me to pray and sing thy praise.

HYMN 23.

On Zion's bright and holy mount,
 Through faith I view those volunteers
Whom God has spared on Christ's account,
 And wiped away their falling tears.

No arm could save our fallen race,
 Unless God's law was satisfied :
Christ then unveiled his lovely face—
 To pay the debt, was crucified.

He endured the Cross, despised the shame,
 In dreadful anguish there he prayed—
Hosanna to his holy name,
 The great atonement there he made.

That gloomy garden where he died,
 He gave his life that we might reign ;
The Jews they mocked, their God denied,
 While on the Cross in Gethsemane.

In Gethsemane on Calvary's mount,
  Christ our Saviour kindly said:
" Oh save vile man, on my account!
  Father, forgive them!" there he prayed.

HYMN 24.

Could I explore the heavens above,
  And view those streets of gold,
And see that God of power and love,
  Those gates of pearl behold,—

I should almost forsake the earth,
  And soar to worlds on high,
And quit that land that gave me birth,
  For joys that never die.

HYMN 25.

There is a heaven of vast delight,
  Where saints and angels dwell;
Where endless day excludes the night,
  Secure from death and hell.

There is a heaven in yonder skies,
Where Christ our Saviour reigns:
There joy and pleasure never die,
And angels sing in sweeter strains.

That heaven I oft times hope to see,
And tune those harps of gold,
Yet still I fear 'tis not for me
Such pleasures to behold.

Ah, could such heavenly joys be mine,
Before my Maker's face,
My heart and will I would resign
To Christ our hiding-place.

HYMN 26.

When I survey my mortal frame,
And view the brittle thread of life,
And think how Christ for man was slain,
How can I harbor sin or strife?

That God that did my soul retrieve,
  From Satan's rage and dark despair,
I must no more his spirit grieve,
  Or trample on his love and care.

Then, when with anxious heart I view
  Those slippery paths my feet have trod,
I fain would bid my sins adieu,
  And cleave to Christ the son of God.

Then when my race and course are done,
  When death shall blast my mortal face,
Give me Salvation through thy son,
  That rock my only hiding-place.

HYMN 27.

Am I a mortal doomed to die,
  And then appear before my God?
Show me the path and hear my cry,
  The path thy Son in glory trod.

The way the holy prophets went,
  The Lord's highway of holiness,
The way to life and pure content,
  The narrow path the road to bliss.

The righteous way from dark despair,
  Where Satan's feet have never trod;
No vile apostate enters there,
  Before that wise and holy God.

HYMN 28.

Burthened with sin and slavish fear,
  To Thee, oh God! I make my moan;
Protect me with Almighty care,
  And kindly guard me as Thine own.

Could I but find my God's embrace,
  And feel my Saviour's dying love,
At last behold His sacred face,
  His mercy-seat in worlds above.

Should Earth and sin my soul oppose,
  And Satan all his powers engage,
Christ sung the triumph when He rose,
  He conquered Hell and Satan's rage.

In that bright Heaven beyond the skies,
  One day I hope to rest my soul
In scenes where pleasure never dies—
  How sweetly must the moments roll.

HYMN 29.

A View of God's Omnipotent Power.

Great God, who rules the Heavens above,
  Directs and bids the planets roll,
Oh, guard me with Thy tender love,
  Forgive and save my dying soul.

Oh, teach me in this dark abode
  To know and do Thy holy will,
Direct me in that heavenly road—
  The path that leads to Zion's hill.

Then teach my wicked heart to pray,
  And take the Bible for my guide ;
Keep Thy commands from day to day—
  Forsake my folly, sin and pride.

Oh, take my heart and seal it Thine,
  Prepare me for Thy courts above :
Thy glorious rest will then be mine,
  To shout and sing Thy wondrous love.

Thy boundless wisdom, love divine,
  Thy plan to save the human race,
My heart and will I would resign,
  To find in Thee a hiding-place.

Thy precious promise doth remain,
  Thy mercy free to all is given :
That precious prize I would obtain,
  To meet with all the Saints in Heaven.

To God, the Father, I will pray,
  That He, through Christ, my soul would
    save :
I'll bear my Cross from day to day,
  For hopes of bliss beyond the grave.

HYMN 30.

Salvation! oh, what scenes of bliss!
  Where living waters ever flow—
How can my Saviour grant me this,
  While I pursue the road to woe.

While I pursue and stand afar,
  And fear to see His sacred face,
That lovely, bright and morning star,
  Clothed with majesty and grace.

Could I but with my God commune,
  With love supreme from day to day,
Drear Winter then would seem like June,
  And I march boldly on my way.

HYMN 31.

How slow to anger is our God—
  To all the works of His own hands,
He spares the chastening of His rod,
  While we neglect His great commands.

He still invites us all to come,
  Forbears to strike the final blow
That seals our great eternal doom,
  In heavenly joy or endless woe.

His powerful arm with mercy shines,
  His ear attends our feeble cry,
He cheers the sad, the sinking mind,
  And says—"Give ear, why will ye die?"

Now whilst our lamp holds out to burn,
  While Christ is on His mercy seat,
May we with faith and love return,
  And ask for mercy at His feet.

HYMN 32.

I hope to see my Maker's face,
  And bow before His throne—
To know His mercy, love and grace,
  And claim Him as mine own.

I hope to wear that starry crown
  That Saints and Angels wear—
With Abram, Isaac, there sit down,
  Freed from sin and care.

I hope to wear that glittering robe
  That monarchs never wore—
To dwell with Thee, like faithful Job,
  On that celestial shore.

I hope to see that Holy Land,
  The Son and Holy Ghost,
And there be placed at God's right hand,
  With all that Heavenly Host.

HYMN 33.

Hinder Me Not.

"Hinder me not!" but let me go
  And do my Master's will,
His goodness, grace and mercy know,
  And all His laws fulfil.

"Hinder me not!" I must go on,
  That heavenly way pursue,
Where my eternal all has gone—
  Methinks his track I view.

"Hinder me not!" I must go on
  To see that glorious place
Where Christ, the King of Glory's gone,
  And bow before His face.

"Hinder me not!" but go with me
  To scenes of joy above,
Those bright, celestial courts to see,
  Where all is peace and love.

"Hinder me not!" I must remove
  To scenes of bliss on high,
Where all is glory, joy and love,
  With Christ forever nigh.

"Hinder me not!" while I shall pray:
  Lord, suffer it so to be,
To do Thy will from day to day—
  At last Thy face to see.

"Hinder me not!" shall be my cry:
 Though Satan's darts be hurled,
I'll bear my Cross, myself deny,
 And face a frowning world.

HYMN 34.

There is a God in yonder skies
 Who hears the prayers of all his Saints,
And sinners, too, whene'er they cry,
 He kindly hears their sad complaints.

When sinners pray with fervent prayer,
 And ask the Father to forgive,
He hears their cry with tender care,
 He says—"Believe, thy soul shall live."

"Believe in Christ, the corner stone—
That stone the builders did deny :
There make thy great petition known—
Believe in Christ, why will ye die ?"

Should sore temptation cast you down,
And Satan's fiery darts be hurled,
God says : "Press on and have the crown
Thy head shall wear in yonder world.

"Thy soul in glory there shall be,
No sin thy heart or mind control ;
With Christ, My Son, to reign with Me,
There, while eternal ages roll."

HYMN 35.

Great God ! to Thee I make my vow,
Through Christ I make this great appeal,
Unless Thine arm supports me now,
A wounded conscience I must feel.

Wounded by sin and sore neglect,
  Neglect my only hope of Heaven,
What I deserve I must expect,
  Unless through Christ I am forgiven.

Through Christ's atoning blood I pray,
  Oh, cleanse my soul from sin and shame,
Show me the path, the good old way,
  Teach me to fear Thy holy name.

Come, Holy Ghost, with love divine,
  Prepare my soul for heavenly bliss,
Renew this sinful heart of mine,
  Lord, grant Thy children hopes like this.

HYMN 36.

It is appointed unto all men once to die. After death, the Judgment. HEB. 9, 27.

Great God! is this my solemn doom,
  That I must die and pass away,
My last remains laid in the tomb,
  My soul appear at Judgment day?

And there before Thy face must stand,
  And have my final sentence given,
Waiting with fear Thy just commands,
  Depart, or dwell with Thee in heaven?

That solemn sentence passed on me,
  To bloom awhile—then fade and die!
May I so live through faith to see
  Thy shining courts in yonder sky.

There I would rest my weary soul,
  And sing Thy praise with all the blest,
No fear of death my thoughts control,
  No sorrows harm my peaceful breast.

Thy Son was slain, mankind to save:
  How can my heart so slothful be?
To pay the debt His life He gave
  In pain and anguish on the tree.

Thy righteous judgment I confess,
  I'll praise Thee for probation given;
That love unfeigned I would possess,
  And walk the path that leads to heaven.

Then may my soul walk fearless on
  That happy road, the way to bliss,
Where my eternal all has gone—
  What can be worth a hope like this?

HYMN 37.

Our Saviour's Cross when I survey,
  And view those pangs for me he bore,
My heart resolves from day to day,
  To try to serve Him evermore.

Those dying pangs He bore for me,
  His hands and feet nailed to the wood,
Those cruel Jews rejoiced to see,
  While round His Cross reviling stood.

A crown of thorns His temples bore,
  His drink was vinegar and gall;
While I recount his anguish o'er,
  Methinks I hear His dying call:

"Repent, oh man! give ear to Me,
  Since on the Cross for thee I died;
I gave My life upon the tree,
  And here behold My wounded side."

HYMN 38.—Luke, Chap. 11—V. 13.

Good Will to Man.

Good will to man I now proclaim!
  The Son of God from glory came,
He brought salvation from above,
  And sealed it with His dying love.

Good will to man I now proclaim:
  Believe in Christ and own His name—
Prepare thyself for heavenly bliss,
  To wear a robe of righteousness.

Good will to man and peace on Earth,
  Was sang in Heaven at Jesus's birth:
Bright Angels left their Maker's throne,
  To make the joyful tidings known.

Good will to man I now proclaim—
   Christ Jesus born in Bethlehem,
The Son of God, the Great Messiah,
   Foretold by John and Jeremiah.

HYMN 39.

Should sore temptation cast me down,
   And grief and sorrow both be mine,
I hope to wear a righteous crown
   That will the dazzling sun outshine.

I hope to feel, to know, and say—
   The Lord directs each bitter cup,
And bear my Cross from day to day,
   And cleave to Him, my only prop.

To feel and know the joys of Heaven,
   Be my whole aim while here below—
To ask and pray to be forgiven,
   Then after death to glory go.

Then will my soul with vast delight,
  See those grand, celestial plains—
There view my Maker clothed in light,
  Where Jesus dwells and glory reigns.

HYMN 40.

When I survey that awful state,
  Of man condemned to endless woe,
I fear lest I should be too late,
  His grace and mercy thus to know.

We should no more presume or dare,
  While fiery billows roll below,
That path of sin to travel there,
  Where Satan and his armies go:

That wicked path of foul deceit,
  Down to the regions of despair.
Oh, Lord! direct and guard my feet,
  Pray, never let me enter there.

HYMN 41.

Come, Holy Spirit, from above,
With Thy Almighty power:
Come, now impart a Saviour's love,
And sweeten every hour.

Don't grieve the Spirit of the Lord,
But lend a listening ear;
His hand can give that great reward—
His word our spirit cheer.

The God of Wisdom is His name,
Eternal power attends His word:
To-day, as yesterday, the same,
No variation in the Lord.

I would with heart, with soul and mind,
Set out anew to serve the Lord;
May I His grace and mercy find,
And sing His praise with sweet accord.

HYMN 42.

Prayer—the Christian's daily food,
  A guide to our Emanuel's land;
It shows us that immortal road
  That leads to God and His right hand.

Prayer—that precious gift from Heaven,
  Whereby we intercede with God:
Through faith in Christ we are forgiven,
  And walk the narrow, happy road.

Prayer—the path the Saints have trod,
  Who now sing praises in the skies:
Before that great, Eternal God,
  In sweet accord their voices rise.

Christ in the gloomy garden prayed,
  Enough to melt a heart of stone:
"Oh, Father! may this cup depart—
  Yet, nevertheless, Thy will be done."

HYMN 43.

When night had spread her sable veil,
  All nature hushed in silent rest,
The powers of Hell could not prevail,
  I then to God my sins confessed.

Those wicked powers so oft have tried
  To lead my wandering feet astray,
At times through faith I have denied,
  And tried to find the good old way.

The way the holy prophets went.
  That narrow path that leads to Heaven,
The road that leads from banishment,
  Where all that walk must be forgiven.

I hope through faith and humble prayer,
  With strict obedience to His laws,
To find my heavenly mansion there,
  To see the last and great first cause.

HYMN 44.

Whilst in the days of health and youth,
  Trust in the Lord, embrace the truth,
Then at that last and awful hour,
  He will guard us with His power.

Our years on Earth will soon be done,
  If we should live three-score and ten,
Death like an avalanche may glide,
  And cut us off in youth and pride.

Then while this throbbing heart shall beat,
  We should live humble at His feet;
Then when our pilgrimage shall end,
  To that bright Heaven we shall ascend.

To shout and sing before His throne,
  In joy supreme before unknown;
That heavenly host in anthems join,
  And sing the song that's so divine.

The song of Moses and the Lamb,
All glory to the Saviour's name,
Who brought salvation from the skies,
And died for man, a sacrifice.

HYMN 45.

When I deplore my wretched state,
Methinks I hear my Saviour say:
" Come now, before it is too late—
Look unto me, I am the way.

" Look unto me and pray in faith,
For if ye ask ye shall receive ;
These words to man My Father saith,
To all the world that will believe."

" Look unto me!" the Lord has said,
From here to Earth's remotest bounds,
" Partake My heavenly banquet spread,
Prepare to see those holy grounds.

To walk those bright, celestial streets,
In Paradise where glory reigns—
In scenes of bliss and love complete,
To sing free grace in joyful strains.

HYMN 46.

August and awful is Thy bar,
Oh, Thou wise and Holy God!
Thy power we see in every star,
All nature speaks Thy name abroad.

Righteous and Holy is Thy throne,
And boundless is Thy love and grace;
The Heavens and Earth are all Thine own,
Pray let us see Thy sacred face.

Thy boundless wisdom has prepared
And spread for man a nobler feast;
If we repent we shall be spared
To dwell with Christ, our great High Priest.

Thou King of Kings and Lord of all,
  The great, first cause of all below,
We at Thy throne for mercy call—
  May we Thy great salvation know.

HYMN 47.

Behold, how Christ our Saviour bled,
  On Calvary's mount He died:
"It's finished now!" He kindly said—
  Here Christ was crucified.

Behold the place with solemn thought,
  Where Christ the Lamb was slain;
Our pardon there He dearly bought,
  That we with Him might reign.

Strict justice by His blood was staid,
  The Saviour died for all;
For man upon the Cross He prayed,
  And left that solemn call:

"Repent, oh man! believe in me,
Remembering where I died;
Behold the Cross, the cruel tree
Where I was crucified."

HYMN 48.

A new Commandment give I unto you, that ye love one another. JOHN 13, 34.

Firm on the Gospel pillars stand
The Saviour's last and great command:
"Love one another!" He kindly said,
"Have faith in me—be not afraid.

"Here hang the Law and Prophets, too,
This great command I give to you,
To reign in Heaven through endless day,
My mandates here you must obey."

With love and grace the Saviour came,
Hosanna to His holy name;
Our souls from Hell He did redeem,
Salvation was His glorious theme.

"Love one another!" he said to all—
 This was His last and dying call:
"Now walk in love here, hand in hand,
 And keep this last, My great command."

HYMN 49.

Remember thy Creator in the days of thy youth. ECCL. 18, 1.

To little children Christ has said:
 "While in thy young and tender years,
Have faith in Me, be not afraid,
 I'll soothe and banish all thy fears."

So I must read His sacred truth,
 Improve my young and tender mind;
Fear my Creator while in youth,
 That gracious God to me so kind.

Oh, teach my feeble mind to pray,
 Direct me in my youthful days
To mind Thy precepts day by day,
 Teach me to love and sing Thy praise.

My youthful days will pass away,
  And vanish like the morning flower;
Learn me while young to watch and pray
  To God to guard me with His power.

May I remember Christ who died;
  While young, prepare to meet my God;
Show me the path, and be my guide,
  The path my loving Saviour trod.

Should I be spared to riper years,
  Great God! direct me here in life;
Guard me secure from all my fears;
  Keep me from envy, sin and strife!

And when my mortal days are past,
  My journey here on Earth is o'er,
May I prove worthy here, at last,
  To dwell with Thee forever more!

HYMN 50.

Three things, oh God! pray let me learn:
Thy love, Thy mercy, and Thy grace;
And while my lamp holds out to burn,
Prepare to see that holy place.

Oh! let me learn Thy sovereign power,
Thy holy mandates to obey:
Guard and direct me every hour;
Show me the bright and holy way!

That joyous path, that righteous road,
That great highway of holiness,
To yonder Heaven, our God's abode,
Where Angels dwell in perfect bliss.

What glorious thoughts my mind pervade,
While I survey God's mighty plan,
And think how justice has been staid,
To save the fallen race of man!

HYMN 51.

May the Lord of compassion, of mercy and love,
Look down from His throne, and pity our case!
Look down from the regions of Heaven above,
And let us rejoice in the smiles of His grace!

Ah, why should I wander, an alien to God,
And feed on the failings of those who profess,
When there lies the path that our Saviour has trod?
All those who walk humbly, he surely will bless.

Christ offers me pardon for all that is past,
If I will embrace Him and cleave to His Word;
And if I prove faithful, and endure to the last,

A crown of bright glory at the right
hand of God.

Such joys are unbounded in every degree ;
No mortal on Earth could ever contain ;
I would with my Saviour in Paradise be,
And there in His presence forever remain.

HYMN 52.

When I shall read God's Holy Word,
And sing to our ascended Lord,
Soft and sweet that strain will be,
Christ Jesus, when I sing to Thee!

Thus while I sing of Calvary's mount,
Where Jesus died on man's account,
Those thoughts affecting still must be,
While thus I sing of Calvary.

Now while I view the path He trod,
  And marked the way with His own blood,
My inward power shall all combine
  To praise a name that's so divine.

But oh, alas ! my wicked heart
  Oft from His precepts doth depart ;
Yet still, at last, I hope to see
  His face through all Eternity.

HYMN 53.

Oh, sinful man ! come, lend an ear,
  And hear what I shall say :
Who dwell in sin and slavish fear,
  Come choose the better way.

Believe in Christ, the sinner's friend ;
  He'll wash away your stain ;
Forsake thy sins ; on Him depend,
  Eternal life to gain.

Have faith in Christ, and hear His voice,
And pray to be forgiven ;
With Saints and Angels then rejoice,
With Him above in Heaven.

With love and fear approach His name,
Confess our sins before His face ;
To rich or poor He is the same ;
He'll save us with His boundless grace.

HYMN 54.

Shall mortal man presume or dare
To take his Maker's name in vain ?
By Heaven or Earth to curse or swear ?
Lord, save my soul from such a stain.

To swear by Heaven, the Throne of God,
How could we mortals dare presume ?
Thus merit the vengeance of His rod,
Who can our lives and souls consume !

To swear by Earth, that God has made,
  And formed by His Almighty Hand!
" Swear not at all!" He kindly said,
  But mind and keep this great command.

How could my lips presume to swear,
  And spread their awful curses round?
With wicked tongue pollute the air?
  Oh, what a sad and mournful sound!

HYMN 55.

God hath no respect of person. Rom. 9; 11.

To Thee, Great God! all homage due,
  From all on Earth and all in Heaven;
To Heathen, Gentile, and the Jew,
  Remission free through Christ is given.

The day of grace is passing by,
  A call is given to all mankind;
God's trumpet echoes from the sky,
  And warns the stupid, deaf, and blind.

The rich and poor shall hear the call,
  All are the works of His own hands;
The high, the low, the great and small,
  Must learn to keep His great commands.

The bond and free, the colored slave,
  May learn to love and praise his name;
Secure that bliss beyond the grave;
  The Lamb of God for all was slain.

The ransom paid for souls like me,
  The Son of God in anguish died,
Condemned and murdered on the tree,
  By wicked Jews was crucified.

Oh, if my heart was cold as lead,
  My wounded spirit would complain;
Mine eyes the tears of sorrow shed,
  To think how Christ for me was slain!

His pains and anguish ever must
  At times affect my sinful heart;
I'll pray to Him in whom I trust;
  From love like this who can depart?

HYMN 56.

Now, Gracious God ! oh, search my heart,
To me Thy love and grace impart;
Forgive my sins, subdue my pride,
For Thou art God, there is none beside.

Our Great Messiah to Heaven is gone,
He whom we fix our hopes upon ;
If He should hide His gracious face,
How sad and awful is our case.

Should He but guard us with His power,
And keep us in temptation's hour,
Though Satan rage and vent his spite,
Our God will save His heart's delight.

Should we but be our God's delight,
Sure He would guard us with His might;
Should Satan try to turn our feet,
Be firm—his words are foul deceit.

HYMN 57.

Amazed I stood and did not know
  Which way to shun the road to woe,
Until my Saviour kindly said:
  "Come hither, soul, be not afraid!"

Lo! glad I come to Christ, the Lamb,
  The Prince of Heaven, the great I Am,
And there before His mercy seat,
  A tale of woes I did repeat.

I told Him all my sore distress,
  My sin and shame I did confess
Before that God, the King of Saints,
  I freely told my sad complaints.

He heard my cry with love and grace,
  He viewed my sad and wretched case:
Then said "Through faith, thy soul shall live—
  Thy sins I freely all forgive."

HYMN 58.

When I survey Thy mercies, Lord,
And view Thy blessings o'er and o'er,
My passions join in sweet accord
To strive to pray and sin no more.

To sin against that God of Heaven,
Where all my happiness depends,
How can I hope to be forgiven,
Unless I try to make amends.

To sin against that God of Grace,
His Spirit wont always strive with man,
He soon may hide His sacred face,
Oh, then embrace Him while we can,

And try to gain His love below—
Then when we quit this mortal frame,
We shall to joy and glory go,
And shout Hosanna to His name,

HYMN 59.

Oh, Lord! convert my sinful soul,
  Grant me Thy blessing from above,
And all my inward powers control,
  Show me Thy grace and pardoning love.

Give me a place with Thee on High,
  Where joys immortal bloom;
May I prepare before I die,
  And enter while there is room.

'Tis the same God that grants the feast,
  That invites us all to come:
Come to the Fount—the waters taste—
  Partake while there is room.

Our Incarnate God from Heaven He came,
  Our sin and guilt He bore:
Hosanna to His Holy Name,
  Henceforth and evermore!

HYMN 60.

"Go, preach repentance, love and faith,"
These words to man the Saviour saith;
Go, tell the world the tempter's loss,
And preach remission through the Cross.

Go, blow the Gospel trump afar,
Proclaim the news, the morning star.
That star that shone far in the east,
That brings to man the Gospel feast.

Go, blow the trump both loud and shrill,
His Holy mandates thus fulfil;
Go preach His Gospel far and wide,
Tell the whole world the Saviour died.

Go, preach to all my Gospel truth,
Go, warn the aged and the youth,
Go, bear thy Cross to gain thy crown,
And break the powers of darkness down.

HYMN 61.

Oh, Sinner, where will you appear,
 While in your sin and wicked way,
If Gabriel's trumpet you should hear
 Echo the last and final day?

Oh, Sinner, where will you appear,
 If Christ your Judge should call?
Your final sentence then to hear,
 Your great Eternal all.

Oh, Sinner, whither wilt thou go
 To find thy Spirit rest?
No home in Heaven or Earth below,
 No place amongst the blessed.

Come hither! seek the Saviour's face,
 Before it is too late,
And plead the riches of His grace,
 And sit at Zion's gate,

HYMN 62.

Should Earth and Hell my soul oppose,
  And Satan try to spoil my peace,
My Saviour here my sorrow knows,
  And bids those sinful powers to cease.

He gives the weary pilgrim rest,
  While tossed on life's tempestuous wave,
Gives him the mansion of the blessed,
  His Heavenly joys beyond the grave.

HYMN 63.

Burthened with sin to Thee I come,
  Bound to Thy tribunal bar,
Help me to flee Thy wrath to come,
  To worship Christ, the Morning Star.

Make plain to me my wretched case,
  While the paths of sin I tread;
Grant me Thy smiles, Thy saving grace,
  May I partake Thy bounties spread.

Thy bounteous hand my wants supplies,
   Thy power sustains my fleeting breath,
Nothing I need Thy hand denies—
   Oh! save me, Lord, from sin and death.

Nothing on Earth beneath the sun,
   Can fill that empty, aching void;
I would that prize of glory won,
   That Heavenly prize, that great reward.

HYMN 64.

Behold, where God our Maker reigns,
   The Saints arrayed in robes of white;
They sing His praise in joyful strains,
   And tune their harps in pure delight.

There God the Father, God the Son,
   Clothed in majesty and light,
The Holy Ghost, there three in one,
   The Saints, the God-Head's great delight.

With Christ the Holy Prophets reign,
  Apostles, Martyrs, there behold,
Freed from sorrow, sin and pain,
  They dwell in joys that can't be told.

There dwell with God, the King of Heaven,
  Through faith their souls have entered there;
Their souls through Christ have been forgiven,
  And kept by His Almighty care.

HYMN 65.

In tribulation Paul did glory,
  And preached the Saviour crucified;
He told the world that pleasing story,
  He that asks is not denied.

If we ask the lovely Saviour,
  If in faith we shall receive,
He bore the Cross for our behavior,
  How can we longer disbelieve?

How dare we longer live in sin,
And all His counsels still deny?
He offers now to take us in,
While the Ark is passing by

Now the Saviour stands a saying—
"Now repent, return and live:
Ye can come through faith and praying,
He that comes I will forgive."

HYMN 66.

He that feareth God and worketh Righteousness is accepted.

Vain man should ever fear the Lord,
And learn to do His Holy will,
To read and mind His sacred word,
His laws and precepts thus fulfil.

With faith and works may I obtain
Admission there with Him in Heaven,
Through Christ's atoning blood to gain,
That precious Gem to be forgiven.

May I with faith and love be found,
  And fear to offend that gracious God,
In realms of joy I shall be crowned,
  Saved through Christ's atoning blood.

Should I obtain acceptance there,
  My soul in glory then would be
Free from trouble, sin and care,
  And all the Saints and Angels see.

Rejoicing in God's saving grace,
  To sound His praise while ages roll,
Before whom Angels veil their face,
  He came from Heaven to save man's soul.

With joys immortal, love complete,
  In yonder skies that place of bliss,
To shout and sing at Jesus's feet,
  Can I obtain a place like this ?

A place with Thee, Great God, in Heaven,
  And strike those golden harps of praise,
To shout and sing my sins forgiven,
  At Thy right hand through endless days.

HYMN 67.

Meditation on the Great and Last Change of Man.

When I shall quit this Earthly frame,
  And go to God who gave me life,
May I forever praise His name,
  Freed from sorrow, sin and strife :

And there before His smiling face,
  With Saints and Angels sing His praise,,
Rejoicing round that Throne of Grace,
  Redeemed from sin through endless days.

God's wondrous love and saving grace,
  His own dear Son a ransom sent,
Who died and suffered in our place,
  Through Him He calls us to repent.

"Repent," he says, "and thou shalt live
  And dwell in Paradise with me;
Confess Thy sins—I will forgive—
  My face in glory thou shalt see."

May I be made to hear His voice,
  Choose the good part that Mary did ;
Let me not make that wretched choice,
  To live in sin, oh God, forbid.

Forbid it, Lord, that I should be
  A stranger to that God above ;
May I prepare Thy courts to see,
  In that bright world of light and love.

And there before Thy dazzling throne,
  With all the justified sit down ;
Thy Son the wine-press trod alone,
  That man might wear a starry crown.

Do Thou but grant me this request,
  To sing Thy praise on Canaan's shore ;
There dwell in Thine eternal rest,
  While time shall be and be no more.

HYMN 68.

Our lives, how short a midnight dream,
  Pass like the current of the air,
While wealth and riches, all our theme,
  Our minds absorbed in earthly care.

Oh, should the Lord that sways the whole,
  Chastise us with His awful rod,
Kill the body—destroy the soul—
  Forbear, we pray, Thou Holy God.

Oh, Lord! Thou knowest our weak estate;
  We can't exist without Thy power;
For joy or woe, thy sentence wait,
  To bloom or fade at every hour.

Guard us while we sojourn here;
  Teach us Thy grace, Thy love, and power
To pray and worship in Thy fear;
  Prepare us for that final hour.

HYMN 69.

Hov can I longer dwell in sin,
And walk the downward road?
T. mend my ways, I would begin,
And make my peace with God.

The Saviour calls; I must obey,
And seek that heavenly road,
To find the straight and narrow way
That leads to His abode.

My Maker smiles, and bids me come,
And press my journey on,
The way to my eternal home,
Where Christ my Saviour's gone.

How can my heart be slothful still,
Refuse that better part?
Teach me Thy love, Thy Holy will,
And cheer my drooping heart.

How can my thoughts so sinful be,
  My heart so dull and cold;
My mind and will, so prone to Thee,
  In sin to be so bold?

Now, when I view God's mercies o'er
  The present and the past,
I hope to reach fair Canaan's shore,
  And dwell with Him at last.

HYMN 70.

"Judge Not, lest You be Judged."

Oh, judge me not for my belief!
  If the heart is right, I ask no more:
The heir of joy, and not of grief,
  My soul will see fair Canaan's shore.

Judge me not, I say, likewise;
  That must be left to God alone:
Then pray to Him in yonder skies,
  For He will judge and save His own.

Lest I be judged, I must not judge,
  But try to dwell in peace and love ;
And owe no man a party grudge,
  But pray to meet them all above.

Lest I be judged, I will refrain,
  And place my all on God in Heaven ;
And try the Saviour's love to gain,
  And pray through Him to be forgiven.

Christ's mission was the world to save,
  And not to judge the human race ;
So on the Cross His life He gave,
  That we might dwell before His face.

Let us prepare for that great day,
  When all before God's face must stand ;
And there our final Judge will say :
  " Depart, or dwell at my right hand !"

Let no sectarian strife be found,
  For each alone must stand or fall :
Let's search the Scripture, round and round,
  While on His name for help we call.

HYMN 71.

All Wise and Holy, Righteous God,
  Who formed the Earth, the Heavens
    above,
We fear the vengeance of Thy rod,
  Teach us to know Thy grace and love.

We hope before Thy throne to bow,
  And there to worship at Thy feet ;
To do Thy will, Lord, teach us how
  Here, from off Thy mercy seat.

Lord, we own Thy dealings right,
  Yet nature shrinks and disobeys,
While mercy is Thy great delight,
  Oh, how mysterious are Thy ways.

Mercy, thy darling attribute,
  Thy justice holds and wields the rod ;
How dare we mortals thus dispute
  The dealings of that Holy God.

Oh, grant us, Lord, that great desire,
To worship there before Thy throne ;
Oh, warm our hearts with Holy fire,
And there to seal us for Thine own.

HYMN 72.

The Preacher's Farewell.

Farewell, my brethren in the Lord,
My Saviour calls and I must go
To preach my Great Redeemer's word,
While I sojourn on Earth below.

To go and preach the joyful news,
Tell it to Earth's remotest bounds,
To Heathen, Gentile and the Jews,
What a dear Saviour I have found.

Farewell, those youthful children dear,
I am bound for foreign lands ;
May you grow up, dwell in God's fear,
And keep His great commands.

And while I preach from place to place,
  I'll pray for those I left behind;
I'll trust alone in God's free grace,
  To cheer my drooping, lonely mind.

HYMN 73.

Great God of Heaven, remember me,
  And when my earthly course is done,
Though feeble, weak, and small I be,
  May I be saved through Christ, Thy Son.

Father of Mercies, hear my prayer,
  Guide and direct me all my days;
Oh, guard me with Thy tender care,
  And keep my feet in Wisdom's ways.

May I remember Christ who died,
  And pray through Him with faith to
    Thee,
And try that Stone the Prophets tried—
  At last Thy Heavenly mansions see.

Jehovah, teach me how to pray,
  Prepare my heart to do Thy will,
And guide me in that Heavenly way,
  That path of peace to Zion's hill,

Eternal King, I would desire
  To walk that way that leads to life;
Give me a firm and strong desire
  To shun the ways of sin and strife.

Great God of Mercy and of Power,
  Give me a heart and mind to pray;
May I improve each precious hour,
  And bear my Cross from day to day.

And when my course is finished here,
  May I from thence to Glory go,
Freed from sorrow, sin and fear,
  There all Thy blissful joys to know.

And there in Heaven at Thy right hand,
  With Saints and Angels shout and sing
In that abode—that promised land—
  With praises cause the Heavens to ring.

And there to walk those blissful plains,
  And view those streets and gates of gold,
Where the God of Hosts and Jesus reigns,
  Such joys in full cannot be told.

HYMN 74.

"I am the Christ, the promised Lord—
  Believe in me!" the Saviour saith:
"And Heaven shall be your sure reward,
  If ye but come to me in faith.

If ye will come with hearts sincere,
  And lay your carnal weapons down,
Thy woful case I then will hear,
  And grant Thy head a dazzling crown.

Oh, sinful man, give ear to me,
  The inquiring soul is my delight;
My Heavenly mansions thou shall see,
  The Saints arrayed in robes of white."

Oh, could we join that Heavenly throng,
  Fain would our longing passions rise ;
Redeeming love would be our song,
  Beyond the blue etherial skies.

Behold the righteous marching home,
  Redeemed from sin through endless days,
The Saints and Angels bid them come
  In glory there to sing God's praise.

HYMN 75.

Father, we pray through Christ, Thy Son,
  To Thee, to be forgiven ;
Teach us to say " Thy will be done
  On Earth as 'tis in Heaven.

Give us this day our daily bread,
  Our debts wilt Thou forgive ; "
This prayer on Earth our Saviour said,
  That we might pray and live.

Great God, we own the power is thine—
   To Thee all glory give;
Our heart and will to Thee resign—
   We would partake and live.

HYMN 76.

Dust thou art and unto dust thou shalt return. Gen. 3, 19.

Dust thou art, poor feeble man,
   And unto dust thou shalt return;
Thy days, alas, seem but a span—
   Then strive thy future state to learn.

Be wise and make that better choice,
   And choose the road that leads to Heaven,
Give God thine heart and hear His voice,
   And pray through Christ to be forgiven.

Since dust thou art, thou must contend
   With sorrow, pains, and ills in life;
Then pray to Christ, the Sinner's friend,
   To keep you safe from sin and strife.

And when thy days are finished here,
  May this thy happy portion be :
Freed from sorrow, sin and fear,
  And all the Saviour's glory see.

Christ Eternal, Prince of Peace,
  May we Thy grace and mercy know,
And reign with Thee where sorrows cease,
  Oh, guard us safe while here below.

May we Thy precepts keep while here,
  Teach us repentance, faith and love ;
Guide and direct us in Thy fear,
  Show us that path to Heaven above.

Prepare us here for Judgment day,
  Where all the dead, both small and great,
Come forth where God himself shall say,
  And fix their last and final state.

HYMN 77.

Thy Throne of Glory, Mighty King,
  In Thine abode, that Heaven above,
Where Saints and Angels shout and sing
  The wonders of Thy boundless love.

Father of Mercies, God Supreme,
  Oh, condescend to lend an ear ;
Our days, alas, are like a dream,
  Burthened with sin and slavish fear.

Lord, we implore Thy matchless grace
  To save our souls from sin and death ;
As sinners, born of Adam's race,
  We ask it with our latest breath.

Thy grace and mercy don't refuse,
  But pardon all our follies past,
And like that race, Thy chosen Jews,
  Bring us safely in at last.

HYMN 78.

A View of Heaven, or the New Jerusalem.

Who can describe that Holy City,
Where the ransomed dwell on high ?
There dwells the Father, full of pity,
And Christ, the loving Saviour, nigh.

Oh, Heaven ! that holy habitation,
Where the Saints in glory reign ;
The rich or poor, in every station,
Can this prize through faith obtain.

Hail ! ye happy, happy spirits,
Who through faith have entered there ;
That glorious bliss thou shalt inherit,
Freed from sorrow, sin and care.

Hail ! Thou glorious, mighty Saviour !
God of Love and Prince of Peace !
May we obtain Thy love and favor,
Thy kindness cause our doubts to cease.

Who can paint the scenes of glory,
  Where those raptured spirits dwell ?
That Golden City lies before thee ;
  The joys of Heaven no one can tell.

There the Saints and Angels singing,
  And praising God in loudest strains ;
The Heavenly Courts with praises ringing
  Sweet music o'er those Heavenly Plains,

Holy is the God of Heaven ;
  Jesus died mankind to save,
That we through Him might be forgiven,
  His life a ransom freely gave.

Oh ! my heart would oft rebuke me,
  And tell how slothful I have been ;
May I set out anew to serve Thee,
  From this glad hour I would begin.

HYMN 79. Isaiah—Chapter 11.

All flesh, like grass, must fade and die,
  And wither like the morning flower;
We soon may heave that parting sigh;
  How should we view that dreadful hour!

All flesh, like grass, may bloom and thrive,
  Yet fall before the noon-day sun;
The dead and gone were once alive;
  Our course, like theirs, will soon be done.

All flesh may bloom, yet doomed to meet,
  And wither like the blasted rose;
The grave, or robe, or winding-sheet,
  Their last remains in death must close.

We mortals bloom, then fade and die;
  Our souls ascend before His throne,
In glory there to dwell on high,
  Should Christ but claim us as His own.

HYMN 80.

Great God! prepare us all for death;
  Be with us through life's stormy way;
Give us that faith, that praying breath,
  That leads to life and brighter day.

Thy throne of light, Thy heavenly fount,
  Where all may come and share Thy love,
On Zion's bright and holy mount,
  There view by faith the Heavens above.

Thy boundless mercy, Righteous God!
  Offered to all the human race;
All those that read and trust Thy Word,
  Will share the riches of Thy grace.

In vain we mortals toil below,
  For bliss in vain on Earth is sought;
May we Thy love, Thy kindness know,
  In truth to worship as we ought.

HYMN 81.

Great God of mercy, love and power!
  Who made the Earth, the Heavens above,
Be with us in death's awful hour,
  Prepare our souls for light and love.

Prepare us all for that bright world,
  In Paradise with Thee to reign;
When Time is to destruction hurled,
  Our trembling souls wilt thou sustain.

Oh, Lord! protect us through those scenes,
  When Time shall cease at Thy command;
Thy wisdom has procured the means
  To bear us safe at Thy right hand.

If we embrace Thy Son, who died,
  And gave His life, that we might live,
Thy grace how can we be denied?
  Forgive our sins, oh, God! forgive!

HYMN 82.

A View of Heaven.

Who can paint the joys in Heaven,
Or sketch those scenes of pure delight,
When a sinner is forgiven,
And brought from darkness into light!

Shout, ye Saints! now there in glory;
Sing salvation through the sky;
Ye Seraphs! tell that pleasing story,
How Christ for sinners once did die!

Ye myriads! sing and shout Hosanna,
Without cessation, day or night;
Arise, ye Saints! and spread your banner,
For Christ will save his heart's delight.

We read that joy is great in Heaven,
When a repenting sinner flies
To Christ, and prays to be forgiven,
And views God's glory in the skies.

But Satan, with his sly persuasion,
Tries to mar and spoil our peace ;
Watch and guard, with strict evasion,
And Christ will cause our doubts to cease.

Jerusalem, that Holy City,
Permit our feet to enter there ;
View us on Earth with love and pity,
And guide us safe from every snare.

Oh, grant us, Lord ! that Crown of Glory,
In Heaven before Thy face to sing ;
And shout Hosannas there before Thee,
With praises to our Heavenly King.

Such joys with fear we oft would mention ;
Alas ! how can we be denied ?
We will bury strife and all contention,
And view by faith Christ's bleeding side.

HYMN 83.

One evening, while musing on God's mercy
and love,
I viewed his compassion and goodness to
me;
Those scenes of bright glory in the Heavens
above,
Through the plan of redemption, I hope
I shall see.

"I would not live alway," the wise man has
said;
Yet a crown of bright glory we hope to
obtain,
Given us by our Maker, and placed on our
head,
In life-love and glory forever remain.

The thoughts of salvation shall solace those
hours
That God has allotted to me here below,

And help to enlarge and strengthen those
powers,
To fulfil the end my Redeemer to know.

My Redeemer to know in those mansions
above,
To dwell with my Maker eternity round,
And sing Hallelujah, all glory and love,
With anthems of praise make the Heavens
resound.

HYMN 84.

The day will come when I must die,
And go to God, who dwells on high;
Oh, may my Saviour then exclaim:
"Here comes a Saint — I own his name!

"He owned my name in yonder world,
Where all the powers of sin were hurled;
He bore his Cross to gain a crown;
At my right hand he shall sit down."

When pain shall rack this mortal frame,
 Then may I trust in Jesus's name;
And when I pass Death's awful door,
 May I be safe on Canaan's shore!

I soon must pass from hence away,
 And meet the last and final day:
Oh, God! sustain my faith in Thee;
 Let me Thy face in glory see!

When friends stand round my dying bed,
 To hold my hands and aching head,
Oh, Christ! be pleased to take my soul,
 To dwell with Thee while ages roll!

HYMN 85.

Great God of Heaven! who formed the Earth
 Gave every creature life and birth,
Oh, condescend to hear our prayer;
 Let us behold Thy glories there.

Lord! save us with Thy boundless grace,
  Permit us there before Thy face,
Where all the Saints in glory dwell,
  Redeemed through Christ from Death and
    Hell.

Redeemed from sin, in heavenly bliss,
  What could we ask Thee more than this!
Where Jesus reigns and Angels sing,
  Sweet anthems to our Heavenly King.

Hosanna, praise and glory be,
  Great God of Mercy! unto Thee;
From all on Earth, and Saints in Heaven,
  Be honor, thanks and glory given!

HYMN 86.

Could I behold that wondrous tree,
  On which the Lord, my Saviour, died;
He paid the debt, the penalty;
  By murderous Jews was crucified.

He on the Cross the ransom paid ;
He tasted death, that we might live ;
The great atonement there He made,
There asked His Father to forgive.

" Father, forgive them !" there He prayed,
With His last, expiring breath ;
Provision ample there was made,
To save our souls from sin and death.

Christ has redeemed from sin and woe,
By pain and anguish on the tree ;
He that repents, to Heaven may go,
And be forever free.

In Heaven, before the Saviour's face,
Being purchased by His blood,
Rejoicing round that Throne of Grace,
Before that righteous God.

HYMN 87.

Father in Heaven! the Widow's God,
The Christian's Guide, the Orphan's Friend,
Unfold the beauties of Thy Word,
Teach us our great, our final end!

Father of Light! we freely own,
How weak and feeble, frail we are;
Our wants to Thee we would make known,
And pray for Thy protecting care.

Thou God of Jacob! Lord of All!
Before whose altar Kings must bow,
And on Thy sacred name must call;
To do Thy will, oh, teach us how!

Thou Rock of Ages! Source of Love!
How can we longer thus delay?
Show us Thy courts, Thy throne above,
And guide us in that holy way.

HYMN 88.

Could I possess that lamb-like soul
  That Christ, my Saviour had,
My fleeting days I would control,
  And never more be sad.

His love to man — poor fallen man —
  Before he should be lost,
He did fulfil his Father's plan,
  Not minding what it cost.

Now if my life will pay the debt,
  The same I'll freely give;
He shant be lost for want of that,
  Let him repent and live.

Such love as this sure has no bounds,
  No parallel is given;
Before whom Angels cast their crowns,
  And all the Host of Heaven.

HYMN 89.

Swear not at all. Mat. 5, 34.

Shall feeble man of flesh and blood,
  Presume to swear by Heaven or Earth,
In presence of that Holy God
  Who hath preserved him since his birth?

Swear not by Heaven, the Bible saith,
  For that's God's bright and dazzling
    Throne:
But pray to Him with fervent faith
  To guard and save you as His own.

Swear not by Earth, the Scriptures say,
  For that's God's footstool, there we read:
But keep that straight and narrow way,
  And pray for help in time of need.

By Jerusalem thou shalt not swear—
  There dwells our Great, Eternal King;
But pray through Christ to enter there,
  And there the Song of Moses sing.

Thus by Thy Head thou shalt not swear,
God formed thy image with delight;
We cannot breathe without His care,
Or change one hair from black to white.

Who can desire to curse and swear,
Or make such wickedness their theme ?
How could my sinful passions dare
With wicked lips God's name blaspheme

Since God has said thou must not swear,
Forbear, oh man, don't be profane;
Oh, guard thy tongue and lips with care,
And never take God's name in vain.

HYMN 90.

How false, vain man, are all things here,
Like golden dreams of joy they fly—
Our days, our months, each fleeting year,
On Time's swift wings are passing by.

While onward, onward, still we move
  Toward that last and trying hour,
Grant us, oh Lord, Thy pardoning love,
  And shield us with Almighty power.

Keep us from sin and foul deceit,
  From arrogance and haughty pride ;
Direct our mind and guard our feet,
  Let us not faint or turn aside.

Let us pursue that glorious way
  Of Heavenly bliss to glory bright,
And keep in view from day to day,
  That precious gem—the Gospel light.

HYMN 91.

Hark! hear my voice! the Saviour cried:
  For unto you, oh man, I call;
Behold my wounds, for thee I died—
  I am thy Great Eternal All.

Hark! hear my voice! ye fallen race—
  Repent, and make thy peace with God;
If ye would dwell before my face,
  This path the dying martyrs trod.

Hark! hear my voice! do not delay—
  Fulfil my mandates here in life;
I am the Truth, the Light, the Way,
  The Way that leads from sin and strife.

Hark! hear my voice! oh, man of sin,
  Now while the Ark is passing by;
Through faith thy soul shall enter in—
  Turn unto me—why will ye die?

HYMN 92.

High on the Cross the Saviour died,
  While all exposed to public view;
"Father, forgive them," there He cried,
  "For they know not what they do."

The Saviour there in anguish prayed—
  "Father, forgive this murderous host:
It's done and finished!" thus He said—
  He bowed His head, gave up the Ghost.

For us the Lamb of God was slain,
  It was there the Prince of Glory died;
He tasted death, then rose again,
  His Father's name He glorified.

"My task is finished now!" he cried:
  "For man, the ransom I have paid;
Behold my wounds! see how I died!
  Come taste my joys, be not afraid."

HYMN 93.

Great God! before Thy mercy seat,
  We would desire to state our case—
To bow ourselves before Thy feet,
  And plead for mercy through Thy grace.

Before Thy throne we would appear,
  And humbly ask Thee to forgive;
Wilt Thou our sad petition hear,
  May we through Christ return and live.

Before that Wise and Righteous God,
  We plead for pardon through Thy grace
Show us the path Thy Saints have trod,
  Let us behold Thy sacred face.

In that bright worlds where Angels dwell,
  Permit our souls to enter there,
And there Thy love and mercy tell,
  Kept and guarded by Thy care.

HYMN 94.

Christ the Chief Head, the Corner Stone.

On Earth our Saviour was denied,
  He whom I placed my hopes upon :
The Stone that all the Prophets tried,
  To scenes of glory now is gone.

Christ is the Head, the Corner Stone,
  A shadowing rock in a weary land;
He trod the wine press here alone,
  Now dwells in Heaven at God's right
    hand.

This Stone the builders did deny,
  The Jews denied and set at nought;
Let's place our hopes, our hearts, and try
  To live and worship as we ought.

And build our house upon that Rock,
  There winds may howl and billows roar,
We shall be safe and stand the shock,
  While time now is and is no more.

Don't let us build upon the sand,
  Where winds may shake or floods
    destroy;
That Rock thereon Immanuel's land—
  There rest our hope, our heart, our joy.

"I am the Rock," the Saviour saith:
  "Believe on me, ye shall not fail;
Press on!" he cries, "with love and faith,
  And Satan's plans shall not prevail."

Lord, place my feet upon that Rock,
 And guard me safe from every ill;
Teach me to love Christ's chosen flock,
 To know and do Thy Holy will.

HYMN 95.

Great is the Lord, the God of Hosts,
 Who made the Earth, the Heavens above,
Great is the Son, the Holy Ghost,
 All one eternal source of love.

How wondrous was the Father's plan,
 To save from sin and endless woe;
To save that noble creature, man,
 Who now through Christ to Heaven
  may go.

His great Omniscient, powerful Hand,
 That made the sun to shine by day;
The planets move at His command,
 The starry Heavens that God obey.

Great God! we own the power is Thine,
  And hope to dwell in Thine abode;
Our feeble powers we would resign
  To Thee, thou just and Holy God.

HYMN 96.

When death shall end my journey here,
  And all my sorrows have an end,
My friends shall shed the parting tear,
  Wilt Thou be mine eternal friend?

Wilt Thou sustain my mortal soul,
  And take me home to realms of bliss
To dwell with Thee while ages roll?
  What could I ask Thee more than this!

I would repent while here below,
  And gain my Great Redeemer's love;
Then after death my soul will go
  To Heaven as spotless as a dove.

My Maker smiles and bids me come,
The Saviour saith, "I am the way—
The way to Thine eternal home—
The glorious path to brighter day."

HYMN 97.

Look unto me, all ye ends of the Earth, and be ye saved. Isaiah 45, 22.

Look unto me, poor sinful man,
And bow before My mercy seat,
And make thy peace now whilst you can,
Oh, then thy joys will be complete.

Come unto me, the Father saith,
For I am God, there's none beside;
Confess thy sins and pray in faith,
For such as those are not denied.

Poor wandering souls give ear to me,
From thence to Earth's remotest bounds
Come taste my joys, my glories see,
And view thy Saviour's bleeding wounds

All can be saved that dwell below,
  Should they give ear and thus repent:
They can through prayer to glory go,
  By faith in Him whom I have sent.

HYMN 98.

Christ, the Lord, our Saviour's name,
  On Him our hopes of Heaven depend,
To save mankind from Heaven he came,
  The sinner's great and glorious friend.

God sent His Son the debt to pay,
  When man had fell in dark estate;
Then Christ appeared to show the way,
  The road that leads to Zion's gate.

Eternal Goodness, Lord Supreme,
  The Corner Stone, the Great I Am,
Our souls from Hell He did redeem,
  We'll shout Hosanna to His name.

When we repeat the Saviour's name,
What thrilling thoughts of love divine,
To think He once from glory came,
To save this sinking soul of mine.

My feeble tongue knows no restraint,
Nor words can tell His dying love;
He hears the sinner's sad complaint,
Shows him the way to worlds above.

HYMN 99.

A View of the Goodness of God.

When I survey Thy goodness, Lord,
And think how sinful I have been,
My passions say with one accord,
To live anew I would begin—

And try to walk in Wisdom's ways,
And bend my course for Zion's hill,
To pray and serve Thee all my days,
With strict obedience to Thy will.

Could I but see that Holy place,
  And view with joy the promised land,
There see my Saviour face to face,
  To shout and sing at His right hand.

Enough, enough, my soul would say,
  Those joys eternal, how sublime;
How could I lose one single day,
  Or waste away my precious time.

Father of Mercies, guide my feet,
  Teach me the way that leads to bliss;
Hear us while on Thy Mercy's seat,
  Deny us not a boon like this.

Great God of Glory and of Power,
  Keep us from folly, sin and strife;
Be with us in a dying hour,
  Show us the path that leads to life.

And when our earthly course is done,
  Our pilgrimage is finished here,
May we that prize of glory win,
  Our souls be free from every fear.

Through Christ we make this great request,
To sing redemption through the sky,
With Saints in Thine eternal rest,
In scenes of glory far on high.

HYMN 100.

How short our days—our fleeting years
Ride swiftly on the car of time;
Our Saviour smiles to soothe our fears,
And cheer this sinful soul of mine.

Christ and the Father both agree
In one unbounded strain of love,
Eternal wisdom did foresee
That plan to save our souls above.

When Adam sinned and fell from grace,
God showed His great and mighty plan,
The Saviour then unveiled His face,
And gave His life for wretched man.

Man was redeemed from sin and shame,
  Christ blessed and claimed us for His
    own;
For those that trust His Holy name,
  He trod the wine press here alone.

HYMN 101.

Could I but view that glorious place,
  Where all the Saints and Angels dwell,
There view my Maker's Throne of Grace,
  What scenes of Glory I could tell!

There all those heavenly beauties see,
  What wonders then I should behold!
There be with Christ forever free,
  And walk those happy streets of gold.

There view the robes and crowns they wear,
  There see that heavenly glittering host,
To dwell with God, my Maker, there,
  And Christ, the Son, and Holy Ghost.

There view my Maker's Throne of Light,,
  And see my Saviour there above;
Those scenes of joy and pure delight,
  All swallowed up in light and love.

HYMN 102.

Lord, at Thy Temple we appear,
  And bow before Thy mercy-seat;
Burthened with sin and slavish fear,
  Forgive us, now, we do entreat!

Forgive us, Lord! aloud we pray,
  While we before Thy justice stand;
Show us the straight and narrow way,
  The path that leads to Immanuel's land.

Press on! saith Christ: Prove faithful then,
  And lay thy carnal weapons down;
The heavenly host will shout amen!
  Thy head shall gain a starry crown.

March on! saith Christ: With faith to see
  That glittering robe prepared for you;
In glory bright thy soul shall be,
  When thou hast bid this world adieu.

Gird on thy sword; don't be afraid!
  The humble soul is my delight;
Take up thy Cross; be not dismayed;
  For thou shalt walk with me in white.

Before God's dazzling throne above,
  I shall delight to own and bless;
There Saints and Angels dressed in love,
  Those joys complete thou shalt possess.

Where joys immortal Heaven complete,
  Before God's Throne to shout and sing;
There bow and worship at His feet,
  And make those heavenly regions ring.

HYMN 103.

Come, poor sinners ! dark benighted !
  Whom the Scriptures seldom read ;
Your fond hopes may soon be blighted ;
  Come, this day, choose whom you need.

Choose thy bleeding, dying Saviour ;
  He for you hath suffered shame ;
Once He died for your behavior ;
  Return, oh, Man ! and praise His name.

Oh, ye sinners ! pressed with sorrow,
  Hear thy Saviour's dying call ;
Don't delay or trust the morrow,
  But think of thine Eternal All.

Now the Saviour stands a-pleading,
  Before His Father's Throne on high :
There in Heaven now interceding ;
  Sinner, turn ! why will ye die ?

Come, ye sinners, poor and needy!
  Come, and try God's love and grace!
Jesus ready stands to save you;
  What a glorious hiding-place!

Then, come, thou loving, mighty Saviour!
  King Eternal! Prince of Peace!
Come, oh, Lord! and reign forever!
  Then will all contention cease.

HYMN 104.

Now unto Thee, great God of Heaven,
  Who knows our thoughts, our will and mind,
Be honor, praise and glory given,
  For Thou art merciful and kind.

Why should our hearts so slothful be,
  So dull and cold to Thee, our God?
Thy love, Thy grace, Thy mercies free,
  To all who trust Thy Holy Word.

Now, Lord! our great, our firm desire
  We raise to Thee before Thy throne;
Oh, warm our hearts with sacred fire,
  And ever seal us for Thine own.

HYMN 105.

Could I ascend to God on high,
  There bow and praise His holy name,
And sing salvation through the sky,
  There shout Hosanna to the Lamb!

What scenes of grandeur there above!
  To dwell before my Maker's face,
There clothed in righteousness and love,
  And taste the riches of His grace.

That great, that shining host to see,
  Of every nation, tongue, and kin;
To be with Christ in glory free,
  Those heavenly gates to enter in.

Before that great, that righteous God,
Who has His Son a ransom given,
That we, through His atoning blood,
May still escape and fly to Heaven.

HYMN 106.

The plan of salvation for mortals like me,
Who have spent so much time in folly and sin,
How can I expect God's Kingdom to see,
Unless to walk humble I shortly begin !

The plan of salvation, so ample and kind,
To those who would drink of the waters of life ;
The system was formed by an Eternal Mind,
Free from contention, from folly and strife.

Now let us consider and think on our ways,
And try to live righteous and Godly while here ;

And if we prove faithful to the end of our days,
Our joys are immortal, with nothing to fear.

To think of those glories, our happiness then,
When we have obtained the Pearl of Great Price;
We will sing Hallelujah! Hallelujah! Amen!
With no fear of death, of envy or vice.

How can we neglect or turn a deaf ear,
When we think of the glories prepared for the blessed?
Then let us prove faithful and live in Thy fear,
And pray to inherit Thy glorious rest!

Our God will consider our proneness to sin,
And forgive our transgressions when humbly we pray;
To set out anew now let us begin,
And ask for instruction to keep the right way.

And when we have finished our journey below,
When the summer is past and the harvest is o'er,

May we to the regions of happiness go,
  To dwell with our Saviour on Canaan's
    shore.

And there to find favor in Heaven above,
  In a place so celestial, without any end,
To dwell in the regions of pure light and love,
  With God our Creator, and Jesus our
    Friend.

There myriads of Angels are casting their
    crowns,
  And shouting Hosanna! Hallelujah! Amen!
The Saints there in glory, their joy has no
    bounds:
  How can we neglect? I ask you again.

HYMN 107.

While I survey my wretched state,
  And think how sinful here I live,
I fear, alas! I am too late
  To ask my Saviour to forgive.

No costly pearl or gem of gold
  Can buy my soul a place in Heaven;
We by our Saviour's words are told,
  We must repent to be forgiven.

Through Christ, remission is obtained;
  He that doth ask shall still receive;
By faith and prayer this prize is gained:
  How can we mortals disbelieve?

Saith Christ: I called, and ye refused
  To lend to me a listening ear!
This call He made before the Jews,
  Who seemed determined not to hear.

But we, poor Gentiles! hear the call.
  And thus should profit by the same;
Here rests our Great Eternal All:
  Our faith in Christ, the Saviour's name.

HYMN 108.

Christ is the Way, the Truth, and the Life. JOHN, 14; 6.

I am the Way! the Saviour saith,
  Then trust in me — ye cannot fail;
Believe in God, and pray in faith,
  And Satan's arts shall not prevail.

Christ is the Truth! the Scriptures say,
  We must be saved through Him alone;
Take up thy Cross from day to day,
  For Christ will bless and save His own.

Christ is the Light! we often read,
  The Pilgrim's guide, while here below;
A stay and staff, in time of need,
  May we His love and mercy know.

May we His goodness feel and share,
  And mark the path our Saviour trod;
With strict obedience follow there,
  With faith in Christ and love to God.

If we would to the Father come,
  We must approach through Christ who
    died,
And pray for that Eternal Home
  To God, who never has denied.

When sinners pray with fervent prayer,
  God will be pleased, and lend an ear,
And guard them with His tender care,
  And wipe away the rolling tear.

If ye desire to dwell with me,
  Ye must be cleansed, through Christ,
    from sin;
That Righteous City thou shalt see,
  Thy soul, through faith, shall enter in.

HYMN 109.

Through faith, I view that glorious sight;
  Those joys above! pray, who can tell?
That land of love and pure delight,
  The place where Saints and Angels dwell

They sing and shout with sweet accord,
In one unbounded strain of love;
There myriads dwell and praise the Lord,
Before His righteous throne above.

Before our great, all-conquering King,
Before the Lord, the Great I Am,
And make those realms of glory ring,
There shout and sing before the Lamb.

Through faith we view those glories there,
And hope for bliss beyond the grave,
And pray for God's eternal care,
Who has the arm and power to save.

HYMN 110.

One evening I walked to a lonely retreat,
In deep meditation my soul was oppressed,
No mortal could hear the sound of my feet,
For nature was clothed with the mantle of rest.

In humble contrition I knelt there and prayed,
When sins without number appeared to my view;
I feared and I trembled, my soul was afraid,
To ask God for mercy was all I could do.

Said the Lord of compassion, of mercy and love,
"Thy sins, although many, their ransom is paid;
They were paid by thy Saviour, now in glory above—
So gird on thy armor and be not dismayed."

With love and thanksgiving I'll bow at His feet,
And tell my complaints when dangers oppress;
Forgiveness and pardon at His mercy seat,
The soul that asks humbly will ever possess

With humble submission to God I will pray
To dwell in His glory, that Heaven above,
Where darkness and sorrow shall banish away
The place there be filled with His glory and love.

That lonely retreat with its value to me,
No mortal on Earth can ever possess;
I would with my Maker in Paradise be,
And before all the world my Saviour confess.

In deep meditation I oft would be found,
In humble contrition I often would pray,
To dwell in bright glory eternity round,
Oh, teach me submission and show me the way.

HYMN 111.

When I survey God's goodness round,
And view His mercies and His grace,
And hear Salvation's joyful sound,
I fain would hide my sinful face

And think how vile in sin I live,
And walk that wicked way—
How will that God my sins forgive,
Should I neglect or fail to pray?

We must believe and place our trust
  In Thy great and glorious name ;
Oh, God of Wisdom ! Thou art just—
  To day, as yesterday, the same.

It's meat and drink to do Thy will,
  To those that humbly walk with Thee,
And bend their course for Zion's hill,
  In sweet communion there to be.

With faith and joy to sing Thy praise,
  And sound Salvation through the skies,
To sing and shout in brighter days
  With Thee in fairer worlds on high.

HYMN 112.

A View of Salvation.

Salvation ! oh, the joyful sound,
  It has gone to Earth's remotest bound,
And echoes through from pole to pole,
  It cures with joy the sin-sick soul.

Poor, weary souls, who are tired of sin,
  This ark of safety enter in
And make thy peace with God above,
  In that abode of light and love.

In that abode, that joyful ground,
  Where pleasure dwells and has no bound,
Those golden streets, those joyous plains,
  Where Jesus dwells and glory reigns.

Death will destroy this mortal frame,
  So let us trust in Christ's dear name,
Then at that last, that dreadful hour,
  We shall be shielded by His power.

It is appointed here that all must die,
  Our souls ascend to God on high,
There have our fearful sentence given—
  Depart or reign with Him in Heaven.

Oh, may we hear that joyful news
  That was rejected by the Jews ;
Our Saviour, born in Bethlehem,
  Teach us to love and praise His name.

Then at that last and dreadful day,
  When Earth and Time shall pass away,
The Sun and Moon shall be no more,
  Oh, land us safe on Canaan's shore.

HYMN 113.

While I survey Thy goodness, Lord,
  And see how sinful I have been,
How can I gain that great reward—
  Those gates of pearl to enter in.

Oh, could I see the Heavens above,
  My God and all His splendor there,
My heart and soul be filled with love,
  And view the robes that Angels wear.

Their glittering robes, how bright they shine,
  They shout Hosanna all as one;
I would obtain that life divine,
  And sing the triumphs of the Son.

I would march on that Heavenly road,
  And view the glories of the Lamb,
My soul be fed with living food,
  And dwell before the Great I Am.

HYMN 114.

Love worketh no Ill to his Neighbor. Rom. 13, 10.

First, thou shalt love the Lord, thy God,
  With all thy heart, thy soul and mind,
This path the Saints in glory trod,
  The meek, the lowly, and the kind.

Next, love thy neighbor as thine own,
  And watch and guard him as the same;
If dangers press, soon make it known,
  And trust in Christ's eternal name.

Love works no ill,—it can't be found
  Where harm was done through love alone:
Trace it to Earth's remotest bound,
  Yet love and mercy are His own.

The Bible says God loved the world,
When man had fell and gone astray—
Then Satan all his vengeance hurled,
But Christ was sent to show the way.

Love doth fulfil that righteous law,
Where hangs those great eternal ends;
Teach us with reverential awe
To pray and strive to make amends.

Love never will thy neighbor harm,
Nor lead astray those giddy youths;
The watchword, Love, shall give alarm
To guide us in the ways of truth.

Love one another—for God is Love—
This is the message ye have heard:
It's Love that draws our hearts above—
These lines were taken from His word.

If thou wouldst My disciple be,
Ye must have Love, that Love supreme,
Take up thy Cross and follow me,
And show the world thy great esteem.

Love all mankind as of thine own,
  Here hangs the Law and Prophets, too;
These words were spoke by Him alone,
  Keep these commands, Christ says to you.

"Love one another," the Saviour said,
  And walk together hand in hand;
Fulfil the law, be not afraid,
  This is My last and great command."

HYMN 115.

Great God of all on Earth below,
  Oh, how mysterious are Thy ways;
May we Thy great Salvation know,
  And sing Thy everlasting praise.

For man to reign with Thee on high,
  Thy pardoning mercy, gracious Lord,
Thy wondrous love and pitying eye,
  For us secured that great reward.

In yonder Heaven thou hast prepared
For us a mansion far on high;
If we repent we shall be spared
To sound redemption through the sky.

How can we place on Earthly things
Our heart, our joys, our chief delight,
When from our God all goodness springs,
Who gently guards us with His might.

He guards us with His sovereign power,
He loves and chastens when He please,
He keeps us in temptation's hour,
While every aching heart He sees.

HYMN 116.

Hear us, Great God, do not deny,
But pardon all our follies past;
Lend us Thine ear and hear our cry,
And save our dying souls at last.

Help us from sin and endless pain,
  Teach us to do as well as say,
Permit our souls with Thee to reign
  In fairer worlds and brighter day.

Oh, Lord, the ransom Christ hast paid
  To save the fallen race of man,
Before Thy justice could be staid,
  This Thou foresaw e'er time began.

That mighty plan Thou didst foresee,
  Whereby the Sinner could be saved,
To dwell in glory there with Thee,
  By sin no longer be enslaved.

We are through sin condemned to die,
  And then appear before Thy face
In that bright world so far on high,
  Oh, save us with Thy pardoning grace.

Could we but know one half Thy love,
  And view Thy mercies all around,
We fain would be with Thee above,
  To walk that righteous, Holy ground :

And there to walk those golden streets,
  And view the beauties of the place,
Immortal joys, with love complete,
  Before the Father's smiling face.

HYMN 117.

A View of God's Greatness and Kindness.

Great God of mercy and of power,
  Teach us to know Thy sovereign will,
Be with us in that trying hour,
  Teach us to know Thy good from ill.

That righteous place to Thine abode,
  Where joys immortal Heaven complete,
That promised land, that happy road,
  There see Thy throne, Thy mercy seat.

Religion, oh that precious gem,
  Hope, like an anchor to the soul,
That brilliant Star of Bethlehem,
  May He our lives and years control,

That Star that shone far in the east,
  Whom all the Shepherds did adore,
For man has spread a richer feast,
  Eternal joys forevermore.

Eternal joys with love divine,
  While mercy is His chief delight,
Oh, may that glorious theme be mine,
  To sing His praise in pure delight.

In pure delight where Jesus reigns,
  Before the Father, clothed in love,
To range around those blissful plains,
  With Saints and Angels there above.

Before that God, that King of Kings,
  There Christ, His Son, and Holy Ghost,
With harps of gold that region rings
  With anthems from that Heavenly ~~joys,~~

HYMN 118.

A View of Christ.

Christ, the great hiding place for man,
Whom God, the Father, sent from Heaven,
We should embrace Him while we can,
And plead through Him to be forgiven.

Christ, like a fountain full of light,
He left His Father's glories there,
To save a lost world was His delight,
Depraved and sinful as we are.

Christ's anguish there upon the Cross,
He suffered shame and sore disgrace,
His dying pains He counts but dross
That man might find a hiding place.

Christ, our King, the Fountain Head,
He left His Father's realms above,
Came down to Earth our souls to wed,
When moved by pity and by love.

Christ, the Dear Lamb, the sinner's friend,
  Our Advocate and Great High Priest,
On whom our hopes of Heaven depend,
  Now He invites us to the feast.

Christ, the great Author of our faith,
  He pleads our cause before the Lord;
" Give ear to me, vain man," he saith,
  And learn obedience from My word."

Christ, the great friend to all mankind,
  Who healed the sick, the blind, the lame,
He cast out devils, restored the mind,
  All glory to His sacred name.

HYMN 119.

Grace, goodness and mercy, all combined
  To form that wise, eternal plan,
To death the Saviour did resign,
  To save the sinful race of man.

That plan whereby we could be saved,
  Where man may dwell secure from sin,
By vice and fear be not enslaved,
  Those Heavenly joys to enter in.

How could our Saviour so divine,
  Consent to die upon the tree,
To save a sinful soul like mine
  In Heaven through all eternity.

Now if our hearts do still refuse,
  And set at naught the Saviour's love,
The road to death and darkness choose,
  And ask no part with Him above :

Oh, what a wretched, mournful case,
  To view his soul in dark despair,
No hopes of mercy, love or grace,
  Doomed to eternal misery there :

Doomed by that wise and powerful God,
  Who oft has called while we refused,
We shall be chastened by His rod,
  As were the unbelieving Jews.

HYMN 120.

The Lord's Supper Instituted. Mat. 26 *C.*

Christ took and blessed, then broke the bread,
And gave His disciples there to eat;
"This is My body," He kindly said,
Come, sit ye round my mercy seat.

He broke the bread, then poured the wine,
"Give thanks," (and gave to them to drink,)
"These dying symbols are divine—
Now ponder well on what you think.

This is My blood that must be spilt
And shed for many on the Cross,
To free the world from sin and guilt,
And pay the debt or man is lost.

But still, henceforth, I will not taste,
Until I drink with you above;
Keep these things safe—let nothing waste—
Seal these memorials with thy love."

And when they all had sung a hymn,
  They to the Mount of Olives went
To preach remission now begin,
  And tell mankind they must repent.

Saith Christ, "This night because of me,
  The Sheep and Shepherd both must part
They soon shall meet in Galilee,
  With glorious views and lighter hearts."

When Christ had blessed and broke the
    bread,
  He took the cup and poured the wine;
"This is My blood," He kindly said,
  "These things are Holy and Divine."

HYMN 121.

Be firm, my soul, shake off thy fears,
  And view thy Saviour's bleeding side;
He knows thy griefs, he sees thy tears,
  Thy daily wants he will provide.

Come, then, my soul, march boldly on,
  With faith in Christ and love to God,
Where thine eternal All has gone,
  Here lies the path thy Saviour trod,

Love, power and mercy has ordained
  That plan to save the human race,
The path with blood our Saviour stained,
  Then offered mercy, love and grace.

How could a heart of flesh and blood
  Withstand the Saviour's last request—
Then view the kindness of our God,
  Who offers us His glorious rest?

Christ offers mercy, love and peace,
  And rest to our immortal souls;
He bids our aching hearts to cease,
  And every fearful thought controls.

He knows and hears our sad complaints,
  Christ's pitying eye is over all;
He hears the prayers of all His Saints,
  And sinners, too, whene'er they call.

HYMN 122.

Firm as a rock Thy Gospel stands,
  Thy heralds preach the joyful news,
All are the works of Thine own hands,
  The Greeks, the Gentiles and the Jews.

"Go, preach repentance, love and faith,
  Remission now I freely give;"
These words to all our Saviour saith—
  "Look up to me, give ear and live."

Look up to Christ, our great High Priest,
  Who tasted death for sinful man,
And now invites us to the feast,
  The marriage supper of the Lamb.

I view through faith with vast delight,
  Those grand, celestial courts above;
There Jesus reigns in glory bright,
  And there our Maker, dressed in love.

HYMN 123.

LUKE, THE 2D CHAPT.

A decree once was passed to tax all the world,
By Cæsar, the great, a Roman by birth:
On the rich and the poor these taxes were hurled,
From the rivers around to the ends of the Earth.

Up to Bethlehem city then Joseph did go,
And Mary, his wife, for Cæsar they feared,
For the Romans were great and mighty below,
Here Jesus, our Saviour, in meekness appeared.

When the days were accomplished, our Saviour appeared,
Here Mary's first born in a manger was laid,
There Joseph and Mary, no danger they feared,
When the Son was refused they were not dismayed.

Here Shepherds were found a guarding their
sheep,
When an Angel from Heaven before them
appeared;
"Arise!" he said, "quickly awake from your
sleep:"
When the news of the Saviour they joy-
fully heard.

"Fear not!" said the Angel, "glad tidings I
bring,
Good will and great joy I now do proclaim,
The birth of the Saviour forever must ring,
All glory, Amen, with praise to His name."

In the city of David our Saviour appeared,
He was seen by the Shepherds as He lay
in the manger,
That Angel of Glory they loved and they
feared,
When he told the glad news of the won-
derful stranger.

Unto Bethlehem city the Shepherds repaired,

Found Mary and Joseph with the babe lying there;
Rejoicing in full in the news they had heard,
Resolved in their minds the truth to declare.

Now suddenly then great numbers from Heaven,
Singing "Glory to God! Good Will toward men!
To the Father and Son, all honor be given,
Even so let it be, Hallelujah! Amen!"

HYMN 124.

Thou Great, Eternal, Triune God,
Thy powerful Sceptre sways the whole;
Thine arm that wields that awful rod
Has power to save my dying soul.

Thou God of Heaven, Thy promise sure
To all that keep Thy great commands;
Should I until the end endure,
Mine eye shall see those Heavenly lands.

Thou Great and Sovereign Lord of all,
  Thy boundless grace and mercy sure,
We on Thy sacred name would call,
  While life shall be and time endure.

Then oh, my soul, march forth and sing
  The Song of Moses and the Lamb,
Behold Thy great, all-conquering King,
  And shout Hosannas to His name.

HYMN 125.

Great God! Thy power is over all,
  The high, the low, the bond or free,
The rich, the poor, the great or small,
  We owe our life, our all to Thee,

Then oh, my soul, forsake thy pride,
  And bow before His mighty Throne,
And take the Scriptures for thy guide,
  And all my wants to Him make known.

From day to day may I be fed
  On richer food than kings can eat,
Eternal life, that living bread,
  Far choicer than the spices sweet;

In those bright realms in joys complete,
  In one eternal scene of bliss—
There shout Amen at Jesus's feet,
  Such joys as these may I not miss.

HYMN 126.

God said, Let there be light, and there was light. Gen. 1, 3.

"Let there be light!" our Maker said,
  When all was dark as midnight hour;
Then light appeared—the darkness fled
  Before His great, Almighty power.

God saw the light, pronounced it good,
  He made the sun to rule the day,
The earth and seas to give us food,
  What wisdom did our God display.

He made the earth, the seas and heavens,
The moon and stars to rule the night,
To man, those boundless mercies given,
The sun with all its radiant light.

That light that leads us to the truth,
Sure must be paramount below,
A staff to age, a guide to youth,
The Gospel light of Christ to know.

HYMN 127. Romans 14, 11.

Every knee shall bow and every tongue confess
Before that God that dwells in Heaven,
May we His love and grace possess,
And pray through Christ to be forgiven.

That righteous God, our Sovereign Lord,
Who rules the Heavens, the Earth below,
Says in His everlasting Word
That every knee on Earth shall bow.

Kings, Queens and Princes, all the same,
The high, the haughty shall confess,
Must bow and praise His Holy name,
If they His joys would e'er possess.

The rich, the poor, the bond or free,
Will equal stand before the Lord ;
They that repent, His joys shall see,
And sing the triumphs of His Word.

Should we confess before the world
Our dying Saviour, Priest and King,
Our sins will be to darkness hurled,
Our voices cause the Heavens to ring.

HYMN 128.

There on the Cross the Saviour died
To save a sinful world like me ;
His dying pangs, His bleeding side,
Those murderous Jews rejoiced to see,

Those woful Jews, that wicked throng,
  In hopes to hide their sin and guilt,
The Lamb of God they led along,
  And there His righteous blood they spilt.

With staves and spears they stood around,
  While mocking, nailed His hands and
      feet;
His head with piercing thorns they crown'd,
  Then grosser insults did repeat.

High on the Cross the Lord was slain,
  Then darkness o'er the land was spread;
Blood from His wounds there flowed amain,
  Oh, there these dying words He said:

"Father, forgive them," there He prayed,
  The Earth it quaked, the rocks were rent,
Strict justice on the Cross was stayed,
  Remission given if we repent.

Three hours in anguish on the tree,
  The temple vail was rent in twain;
How could my heart endure to see,
  Or read His sufferings o'er again.

He died, the King of Glory dies,
  The great atonement there He made;
"It's finished! now," the Saviour cries,
  "For man the ransom I have paid."

HYMN 129.

Should sore affliction cast me down,
  And pain and sorrow both be mine,
I hope to wear a starry crown
  That will the dazzling sun outshine.

Great God of Heaven! I would adore,
  The Saviour's name may I confess,
When time with me shall be no more,
  Then wear a Robe of Righteousness.

But woe is me should I refuse,
  And thus outstand my day of grace,
While I have power I pray to choose
  To see that glorious, happy place.

Preserve me, Lord, while here below,
Keep me secure from every sin ;
May I that road to glory go,
The ark of safety enter in.

Oh, there to be on that blest shore,
Freed from sorrow, pain or ill;
To shout and sing forever more,
And do my Saviour's Holy will.

HYMN 130.

A View of Man.

When I survey God's glorious plan,
With wonder view His saving grace,
Then view myself, poor feeble man,
And think of Christ, our hiding place.

What pity moved the Father's breast,
He views with love our mournful case ;
He offers now His glorious rest,
Through Christ, our only hiding place.

How could my passions move so slow,
  While time keeps on its rapid pace?
I would Thy grace and mercy know,
  And trust in Christ, my hiding place.

How could my heart on Earth refuse
  His love, His mercy and His grace,
And like the unbelieving Jews,
  Deny the Lord, our hiding place?

I would through fear approach His throne,
  There bow myself before His face,
My wants and troubles there make known
  Through Christ, the sinner's hiding place.

Our case is mournful here below,
  Should we neglect to seek His face;
I would with Saints to glory go,
  Rejoicing in my hiding place.

How could my heart so slothful be,
  And thus outstand my day of grace?
I hope through faith and prayer to see
  In God's abode, our hiding place.

HYMN 131.

Ye heirs of Salvation who are bound to afar,
Who feed on the pastures of love,
And believe in the Saviour, the Bethlehem star,
And press on to regions above.

There myriads of Angels and Saints will rejoice,
When man his dear Saviour is searching to find—
To find his Redeemer and follow His voice,
And leave all their sorrows behind.

To their Saviour in glory their wants they make known,
Through faith, for Salvation they call,
On His grace and His mercy they venture alone,
And trust their Salvation, their all.

Through faith and Salvation I hope I shall see
My Saviour in regions above,

And there with my Maker in Paradise be,
Where all is bright, glory and love.

Oh, there my Redeemer in glory doth shine,
While Cherubims shout and adore;
If courts so celestial could ever be mine,
I never could want nothing more.

Salvation is free to the aged and youth,
To all who His kindness would know;
To those who walk humbly and believe in the truth,
To the mansions of glory may go.

HYMN 132.

Oh, careless sinner, now give ear,
And hear what I shall say—
Your Maker's counsel you shall hear,
Remember the Sabbath day.

That blessed, Holy day of rest,
To man and beast is given,
Whom God, our Father, made and blest,
The best of all the seven,

That Holy day, that blessed morn
   Will guide us on our way ;
May we its great importance learn—
   To mind the Sabbath day.

When to that Sacred church we go,
   Where man is wont to pray,
Thy great commandment still to know—
   To keep Thy Sabbath day.

I would no longer live in sin,
   Lord, teach me how to pray;
With love to thee I would begin,
   And mind Thy Sabbath day.

Blest is the man who shuns the place
   Where men neglect to pray,
He trusts in God, his hiding place,
   And keeps that Holy day.

HYMN 133.

High on His throne our Maker sits,
  In the third Heavens above;
Our feeble race He ne'er forgets,
  But guards us with His love.

Oh, could I climb that Heavenly road,
  There view His throne of grace,
In realms of light, His high abode,
  And bow before His face.

My soul would fain forbear to come
  Back to its mother Earth,
But cleave to that eternal home
  Of joy and solid mirth.

Our Saviour views us here below,
  He claims us for His own;
May we His great salvation know.
  And bow before His throne.

HYMN 134.

Great God ! to Thee before Thy throne,
  We humbly wish to bow ;
With humble souls our wants make known,
  And prove our former vow.

From sin and guilt I would be free,
  My Saviour, teach me how ;
May I Thy courts, Thy glory see,
  And at Thy feet to bow.

Oh, may my heart, my soul and mind,
  From Satan's rage be free,
And pray through faith Thy joys to find,
  Through all eternity.

Through every age that sin and shame,
  By our first parents given—
We would adore the Saviour's name,
  And bend our course for Heaven,

HYMN 135.

The Day of Judgment.

Oh! sinner where, where will you flee,
  When Christ, our Judge, shall call:
Give ear, oh Earth, yield up, oh Sea,
  Thy dead—both great and small.

Then death and hell yield up their dead,
  And each His doom shall hear;
Oh, view that day with awful dread—
  How then will you appear?

Come! sinner, come! and don't delay,
  But make Thy peace with Heaven;
Prepare for that great Judgment day,
  And pray to be forgiven.

While Christ is on His mercy seat,
  Make thy salvation sure,
Prepare that awful day to meet,
  Through Christ to be secure.

When all must stand before the Lord,
  The dead, both small and great,
With trembling limbs to hear His word,
  Their dreadful sentence wait.

Oh! sinner, come! pray don't forbear,
  Oh! then no more delay,
For that dread hour, oh, now prepare,
  That awful Judgment day.

HYMN 136.

He dies, the King of glory dies,
  That dreadful debt to pay;
He on the Cross in anguish cries,
  "Oh! man, give ear, I am the Way."

I am the Christ, the true Messiah,
  That was foretold to be;
Give me that faith, a true desire,
  My Saviour's face to see.

Now, O, my soul, take courage then,
  And place thy trust in God ;
To Jesus Christ we'll shout Amen,
  And spread His praise abroad.

He dies, the Great Redeemer dies,
  The dreadful debt to pay ;
" Give ear to me, O, man," he cries,
  " There is no other way."

HYMN 137.

Repent, for the Kingdom of Heaven is at hand. Mat. 4, 17.

Repent, for God's Kingdom is surely at hand,
  Remission to all now freely is given ;
Be humble and keep His righteous command,
  For Christ is the only true way to Heaven.

Faith and repentance will carry us there,
  To that region of light, that haven of rest,
Free from pollution, from sorrow and care,
  To dwell with our Maker in that city of rest.

God saw from His throne and pitied our case,
With love He invites us to repent and believe,
And always enjoy the smiles of His grace,
His goodness and mercy forever receive.

God searcheth the heart and trieth the reins,
He kindly invites to give ear and repent,
And try to walk humbly while time yet remains,
Be honest and just, with our lot be content.

While goodness and mercy now freely are given,
And the Saviour invites while justice is stayed ;
"Now if ye repent your reward shall be Heaven,"
These words by the Saviour have truly been said.

Grace, goodness and mercy are given us free,
If we but walk humbly and try to do well ;
In the scenes of bright glory we ever shall be,
Safe from corruption, from sorrow and hell.

'hrough faith and repentance, remission is
given
To all who in time the Saviour embrace,
ı the region of glory, the Kingdom of
Heaven,
Hallelujah to sing in the smiles of His
grace.

HYMN 138.

Awake! my soul, come forth and sing
To Christ, my Saviour and my King,
Who guards me with Almighty power,
And keeps me in temptation's hour.

He yet sustains my fleeting breath,
And keeps my feeble frame from death;
May He the inner man control,
And purify my mortal soul.

While God afflicts my feeble frame,
May I the more revere His name,
And while I feel His chastening rod,.
Then say—Amen, 'tis from my God.

Oh, make my Heavenly purpose sure,
  Like pious Job I would endure;
When death shall blast the comely face,
  Give me the riches of Thy grace.

HYMN 139.

The Christian's Warfare.

Should I contend with Satan's rage,
  My General tells me when,
The place and where I should engage,
  I gain the victory then.

My coat of arms shall be His Cross,
  Before His ensign I will bow;
My treasure here I'll count but dross,
  And prove my courage now.

Come! sinner, come! come 'list with me,
  Thy board and wages sure,
As long as time and time shall be,
  Should we the fight endure.

Press on ! press on ! Jehovah cries,
  The victory you will gain,
And conquer him with all his lies,
  Here in this rugged main.

Our troops are all a chosen band,
  Oh, see their banners wave !
We're marching to Immanuel's land,
  With hopes beyond the grave.

"Don't fear ! be firm !" our General cries,
  And gird thine armor on—
To that bright Heaven beyond the skies,
  Where Christ, our Saviour's gone.

HYMN 140. MAT. 19, 14.

"Forbid them not," the Saviour said,
  "But suffer them to come to me ;
Ye Jewels, come ! be not afraid,
  Of such, My Kingdom sure must be.

Be not afraid, I am Thy friend,
  For thou art precious in my sight;
Then pray to God, He will defend,
  Thy youthful souls are His delight.

Forbid them not to come to me,
  My Father loves and guides their feet;
These humble souls My face shall see,
  And worship round My mercy seat.

If thou wouldst My disciple be,
  You must be humble as a child,
My throne of glory there to see;"
  These words He spoke in accents mild.

"Forbid them not—that must not be—
  While mercy is My chief delight;
Those smiling babes shall dwell with me,
  Like stars of gold in glory bright.

Forbid them not—no, that could not be,
  These little souls are free from guilt:
My dying pangs have set them free,
  For great and small My blood was spilt.

Christ took them in His arms and smiled,
  Then claimed them for His own;
In words of love and looks so mild,
  Made His kind mission known.

"Forbid them not," the Saviour cried,
  "For that could never be:
Let them behold My feet and side—
  My wounds while on the tree."

HYMN 141.

'rom the regions of light, from the mansions
    of bliss,
  An Angel descended with joy in his face,
le told the good news, and the fact must be
    this,
  How man could be saved by his Maker's
    free grace.

'he story was told in the regions around,
  How a Saviour was born and He laid in a
    manger;

The Shepherds adored and the wise men the;
found
And believed in their Lord, the wonderfu
stranger.

The news it went forth from the regions c
Heaven,
On the wings of an Angel was carried
afar,
How man through his Saviour can now be
forgiven,
By faith in the Lord, the Bethlehem star.

HYMN 142.

Great God, who formed the Heavens and
Earth,
Then made that noble creature, man,
By him foretold our Saviour's birth,
Then showed Thy great, eternal plan.

That God of Wisdom did ordain,
And now invites us to the feast;
The Lamb of God for man was slain,
Our Saviour and our great High Priest.

Father of Heaven! Thou righteous God!
To Thee we owe our lives, our all;
Forgive our sins and spare Thy rod,
We on Thy name for mercy call.

Parent of Mercy! Thou King of Saints,
Send down Thy blessing from above,
And hear our cries, our sad complaints,
Oh, grant us Thine eternal love.

Give us this day our daily bread,
We pray through Christ to be forgiven;
This prayer on Earth our Saviour said,
To help us on our way to Heaven.

9

HYMN 143.

The choicest food on Earth is love,
  Where man may feed his hungry soul:
Its blessings here, its joys above,
  My nobler passions all control.

My nobler thoughts through love aspire
  To Heaven above, where Jesus reigns;
It fills my heart with pure desire
  To sing His love in louder strains.

'Twas love that viewed our wretched case,
  When man had sinned against the Lord
And in that garden fell from grace,
  Condemned by His eternal Word.

Should we neglect God's Holy love,
  And all His counsel set at nought—
May we return like Noah's dove,
  Our souls the Saviour dearly bought.

That love that moved the Father's breast
  To send the Mighty Saviour down;
That love so pure His Son possessed,
  He wrought for man a richer crown.

HYMN 144.

The Gospel Feast.

The Gospel Feast so richly spread,
  Christ spread the same on Calvary's mount;
To sinful man he kindly said,
  "I'll suffer death on thy account."

Christ spread the feast with love divine,
  With food so choice and spices sweet;
There to the Cross He did resign,
  Nailed to the wood both hands and feet.

"It's finished! now," with joy He cried,
  "I have spread the Feast before them all;"
The Jews they mocked and still denied,
  And refused to hear His dying call.

Christ spread the Feast, the Gospel light,
That gem He purchased with His blood;
To save our souls was His delight,
All glory to the Son of God.

Bright Angels left their glorious sphere
On wings to spread the news afar,
That Jew and Gentile both should hear
Of that rich Feast, the Morning Star.

HYMN 145.

Transcendently high and Holy God,
To Thee, we raise our longing eyes,
To dwell with Thee in Thine abode,
There far beyond those azure skies.

Thou Rock of Ages, hear my prayer,
And condescend to grant relief;
Let us behold Thy glories there,
Forgive us, Lord, our unbelief.

Our unbelief, how great that sin,
May we repent and cleave to God,
To see those streets and walk therein,
Through faith in Christ's atoning blood.

Could we but climb that happy road,
With love and fear approach His throne,
In presence of that Holy God,
Our wants and troubles there make known.

Thy heavenly courts in yonder skies,
Permit our souls to enter there ;
May humble prayer like incense rise ;
Keep us from sin and every snare.

Show us the road and guard our feet,
The way that leads from Earth to Heaven ;
While Christ is on His mercy-seat,
We humbly ask to be forgiven.

To Thee, our King, that Great I Am,
Be honor, praise and glory given ;
All on Earth shall praise Thy name,
The Saints and Angels there in Heaven.

HYMN 146.

The Apostles' Commission. *Mark* 16 : 15.

"Go, preach my Gospel!" saith the Lord,
"With strict obedience to my Word,
To every nation under Heaven:
He that repents, shall be forgiven!

"Go, preach remission, faith and love;
Point out the way to Heaven above;
In heathen lands my truths declare,
And try to spread my Gospel there.

"Go, preach repentance to the last,
Where e'er thy lot by chance is cast;
The Greeks, the Gentiles, or the Jews,
Tell the whole world the joyful news.

"Go, preach salvation through my son,
And when thy earthly task is done,
Oh, then thy soul with me shall reign,
Thy head a Crown of Glory gain!"

HYMN 147.

Make bare thine arm, Almighty God!
   Support my feeble frame;
Teach me Thy Truth, Thy Holy Word,
   And how to praise Thy name.

Thou, oh, my soul! stand forth and sing
   The wonders of the Lord,
And cause those sacred walls to ring
   With warnings from His Word.

Come, Holy Ghost, with Christ divine,
   Help me my voice to raise;
Oh, could such joys on Earth be mine,
   To sing my Maker's praise!

Come, Jesus Christ! that Heavenly Dove,
   Who my transgressions bore,
To save my soul with Thee above,
   Thy limbs were stained with gore!

HYMN 148.

Nations must bow, God's Grace implore,
Kingdoms shall tremble at His Word,
Saints and sinners his name adore,
Or meet the vengeance of the Lord.

Oh, sinners ! before God's powerful hand,
Nations must bow, their homage pay ;
Then try to keep His great commands ;
Come hear His voice, no more delay.

To meet that powerful, Holy God,
And stand before His awful bar,
Merit the vengeance of His rod ;
We see His power in every star.

His power is awful and sublime,
Angels and Arch Angels veil their face ;
The Heavens the dazzling Sun outshine ;
No gold could help adorn the place.

HYMN 149.

In the Third Heavens, our God's abode,
  That grand celestial place,
Could we but climb that heavenly road,
  And view our Maker's face;

There see His Throne, His Judgment-Seat,
  The Saints and all the glittering host,
These worship at our Maker's feet;
  Praise Father, Son and Holy Ghost.

Deny us not Thy sovereign grace,
  But save us all through Christ, Thy Son,
Who at the time unveiled His face,
  Foretold by man e'er time began.

Christ left His Father's Courts on High;
  Amazing pity! what wondrous love!
He came to Earth to bleed and die,
  That we might dwell in Heaven above.

HYMN 150.

How can my soul endure to be
  A sinner to that God above?
I hope one day His joys to see,
  And dwell with Him in perfect love.

I hope to see His gracious face,
  Where all is happiness and peace,
And worship round His Throne of Grace,
  Oh, then will all my sorrows cease.

I hope to wear a starry crown,
  Such gems as monarchs never wore;
With friends and brethren there sit down,
  To want or wish for nothing more.

I hope, through prayer and love, to be
  An humble follower of the Lamb,
To be with Christ forever free,
  And there forever praise His name.

I hope to hear His heavenly voice,
  In tones of love, so sweetly say :
" Come hither, soul, with me rejoice ;
  With faith press on ; I am the way !"

HYMN 151.

The Preacher's Prayer.

Thou King of Glory ! God Supreme !
  Who rules the Heavens, the Earth below,
Thy grace, Thy love, shall be my theme,
  Whilst I a wandering pilgrim go.

Should I be called to preach Thy Word,
  To Gentile, Hebrew, or the Greek,
To bear a message from the Lord,
  May I with love and wisdom speak.

Father of Mercies ! hear my prayer,
  Give strength and utterance to my speech,
May I Thy grace, Thy truths declare,
  While I on Earth shall live to preach.

Clothe me with wisdom, grace, and love,
And while I preach from place to place,
Grant me that power from Heaven above,
To preach the riches of Thy grace.

Lord, when I preach Thy Gospel truth,
Send forth Thy Word to every heart,
To age, to middle age, and youth,
The Bread of Life wilt Thou impart?

Then, when my task is done below,
My mission finished here in life,
May I to realms of glory go,
Beyond the power of sin and strife.

HYMN 152.

Sinners, come hear thy Saviour's voice,
No more deny his name;
Then all within thee will rejoice,
And feel that heavenly flame,

Sinners, come trust His Holy Word,
  And thus implore His grace ;
Believe in thy ascended Lord,
  And bow before His face.

Sinners, give ear, no more delay !
  Make thine election sure,
And try to keep that good old way,
  Like soldiers to endure.

Sinners, give ear, and hear me tell
  How Christ, your Saviour, died ;
And how he conquered Death and Hell,
  Salvation to provide.

HYMN 153.

Behold, the Lamb of God was slain,
  He suffered death that we might live ;
Now let us trust in His dear name,
  All honor, praise, and glory give.

Endured the Cross, despised the shame,
  Bound in chains the monster Death,
To glorify His Father's name,
  He died, and yielded up his breath.

Resolved to do His Father's will,
  Prompted by pity and by love,
His dreadful mission did fulfil,
  That we might dwell in world's above.

In perfect bliss, at God's Right Hand,
  Where Angels bow before his face,
Could I but see fair Canaan's land,
  And view the glories of the place.

HYMN 154.

Eternal God! Thou King of Kings!
  Before whom Angels veil their face!
With harps of gold that region rings,
  With praise around Thy Throne of Grace

Could we but view Thy sovereign power,
And realize Thy bounties given,
We should improve each fleeting hour,
To make our peace with Thee in Heaven.

How hard our hearts, how cold to Thee !
Forgive us, Lord, our unbelief;
May we Thy face, Thy glories see ;
Oh, send our minds Thy kind relief !

Great God ! Thy promise, ever sure,
To those who read and trust Thy Word ;
The humble soul is here secure,
And holds communion with the Lord.

HYMN 155.

On Jordan's stormy banks I stand,
And view the prospect all around,
And see by faith that Promised Land,
That happy place of Holy Ground.

That happy place of pure delight,
  Where Saints Immortal shout and reign ;
Those golden streets, that joyous sight,
  That Heaven I oft times hope to gain.

To view that place, that happy land,
  The Saints arrayed in robes of white ;
There Angels bow at His command ;
  What scenes of glory to our sight.

There joy and glory have no bounds ;
  There Seraphs fly across the plains,
To dwell with Christ while ages round :
  Afflictions here I 'll count my gains.

HYMN 156.

How oft would I cherish those fond hopes of seeing
  My Saviour in Glory, in regions above ;
My Maker in Heaven, that Just, Holy Being.
  Dressed in compassion, in glory, and love.

How can we be slothful, while Christ is
a-pleading
With us to repent in the days of our youth?
In the regions of love He is now interceding,
He invites us to come and believe in the
truth.

I cannot forget Him who purchased my pardon,
In courts there celestial His face I would
see;
He was nailed to the Cross in that dread,
gloomy Garden,
There in anguish He died for sinners like
me.

HYMN 157.

Oh, sin! the cause of all my grief!
The cause of my Redeemer's death;
To save the world and give relief,
For man He yielded up His breath.

He dies! the Friend of Sinners dies!
  For them his righteous blood was spilt;
He made that woful sacrifice,
  To save our souls from sin and guilt.

Then, Friend of Sinners, hear me call!
  And pardon all my sin and guilt;
Here rest my Great Eternal All,
  If on the rock my house is built.

If I should build upon the sand,
  Where winds may howl and billows roar,
I ne'er shall see that happy land,
  Nor rest my soul on Canaan's shore.

HYMN 158.

Thou God of Jacob, hear my call,
  Oh, lend to me a listening ear;
My case is mine Eternal All,
  Oh, Lord, forgive and soothe my fear.

I hope through faith and prayer to be
  A servant of the living God ;
Thy courts, Thy Heavenly mansions see,
  And walk the streets Thyself hath trod.

Come ! sinner, come ! embrace the Lord,
  And view His mercies o'er and o'er,
Then Heaven shall be Thy great reward,
  Thy soul shall land on Canaan's shore.

When thou shall move to yonder world,
  Thy soul on Angels' wings be borne,
Thy sins to outer darkness hurled
  Thy soul no more to weep or mourn.

HYMN 159.

No thought can reach, no tongue declare,
  The glories of our Maker, God ;
No finite soul can enter there,
  Unless through Christ's atoning blood.

We must be cleansed from every stain
   From sin by our first parents given,
For us the Saviour once was slain,
   The only way, our guide to Heaven.

Our guide, our lamp, our beacon light,
   Our Head—the Fount of all our joys,
While mercy is His chief delight,
   His presence all our grief destroys.

HYMN 160.

God saw from off His dazzling throne,
   We mortals here condemned to die;
He made His great, kind purpose known,
   He viewed us with a pitying eye.

'Twas then the Gospel feast was spread,
   The great Messiah had come to Earth,
Then tears of joy by Saints were shed
   At Christ, our great Redeemer's birth.

The great Messiah has come to reign,
  Who was, and is, and is to be ;
His Father's glory did sustain,
  For man He died upon the tree.

And now He stands with open arms,
  Inviting all of us to come,
With palms of victory in His hands,
  Over Death, Hell and the tomb.

HYMN 161.

Help me now, oh righteous God,
  In this most trying hour;
Help me to preach Thy Holy Word
  With pungency and power.

Help me with fear and Holy awe,
  To preach Thy great, important truths ;
And from Thy Sacred Scriptures draw
  Some rich instructions to our youths.

Help me while I am called to preach,
  To preach repentance through Thy Son;
Help me Thy Gospel truths to teach,
  To warn them of Thy wrath to come.

Help me to practice what I preach,
  To mind and do as well as say;
The riches of Thy Gospel teach,
  And guard my feet, don't let me stray.

HYMN 162.

Thou Rock of Ages! King of Heaven,
  We on Thy sacred name would call
Through boundless grace to be forgiven,
  There rests our great Eternal all.

In sin and thraldom here we live
  And walk our wicked ways;
Through Christ, Thy Son, wilt Thou forgive
  And thus prolong our days.

Don't cut the brittle thread of life,
  But still my Earthly frame preserve ;
Though laden with sin and foolish strife,
  Deal not with me as I deserve.

May I, through deep repentance find
  Favor in my Maker's sight,
And trust His grace, His precepts mind,
  To do His will be my delight.

HYMN 163.

Thou King of Heaven, the sinner's hope,
  We rest on Thy Almighty power ;
How can we sink with such a prop,
  That keeps and guards us every hour.

That God that bids the planets roll,
  Bids each its course in order keep ;
His arm has power to save my soul,
  His watchful eye can never sleep.

Before that great, all-searching eye,
Our actions good or ill are known;
He sees from Heaven, in yonder sky,
Looks down from His Almighty throne.

His power is awful and sublime,
No flesh can stand before the Lord,
His promise sure and so divine,
We'll rest our all upon His word.

HYMN 164.

To that bright Heaven in yonder skies,
May all my noble passions rise;
That blest abode where Jesus reigns,
To sing His love in sweeter strains.

With songs and anthems sing His praise,
Through boundless years and endless days,
In joy complete my raptured soul,
To sing His praise while ages roll.

There worship round our Saviour's feet,
  In joys immortal, love complete,
While Angels strike their golden lyre,
  And fill our soul with sacred fire.

With fervent love and heavenly zeal,
  May I Thy goodness know and feel;
Do Thou Thy grace to me impart,
  And print Thy laws upon my heart.

Direct me to that heavenly hill,
  Thy glorious purpose to fulfil;
And when I pass Death's iron gate,
  May angels for my spirit wait;

To waft my soul to realms above,
  And there to sing redeeming love;
To see my Saviour face to face,
  And worship round Thy Throne of Grace.

HYMN 165.

Come, sinner! come! thy soul prepare,
  To see thy Saviour's glories there;
And when thy course is finished here,
  To meet with joy and not with fear.

To meet thy Saviour in the skies,
  To run the race and win the prize,
To gain a Robe of Righteousness,
  And all those Heavenly joys possess.

By meek repentance, faith and love,
  To dwell with Christ in Heaven above,
Before that grand, that Heavenly Host,
  Sing praises to the Holy Ghost.

Come, sinner! come! no longer wait,
  For fear thy prayer should be too late,
While Christ is on His mercy seat,
  Come, sinner! bow before His feet.

HYMN 166.

Should sinful man presume to be
  More Holy than his Maker, God?
If he his awful case could see,
  His soul would sink beneath the load.

Laden with guilt and heavy woes,
  He walks the road to dark despair;
His Saviour calls, while on he goes,
  To search for bliss he knows not where.

To search for bliss and joy below,
  Is like a false, an idle tale;
How can my passions move so slow!
  While there is hope I shall prevail.

Hope, like an anchor to my soul,
  Hope bears my sinking spirit up;
Do thou, oh God! my heart control,
  And be my stay, my only prop.

HYMN 167.

Salvation! oh, that Heavenly voice,
  It makes my heart, my soul rejoice;
My inward passions all combine
  To sing a song that's so divine.

Salvation! oh, the glorious news,
  To Gentiles, Greeks, likewise the Jews;
Oh, God! thy healing streams impart,
  And print Salvation on my heart.

Salvation! oh, thy chariot wheels,
  Thy healing balm the sinner feels;
Roll on and spread the news afar,
  The birth of Christ, the Morning Star.

Salvation! oh, the Heavenly theme,
  We pass it like the midnight dream;
How can we slight the Saviour's voice,
  Before whom Heaven and Earth rejoice.

Salvation! oh, thy joys to feel,
  Lord, take my heart and place the seal;
Oh, seal it for Thy courts on high,
  Where joys immortal never die.

HYMN 168.

Go preach Salvation through the Cross,
  Tell the whole world the Saviour died;
While Satan rages at his loss,
  God's Holy Law was satisfied.

Go preach Remission, Love and Faith,
  Repentance through the Son of God;
This is the way the Bible saith—
  The way that John the Baptist trod,

The way the great Apostle Paul
  Besought the Romans to believe;
To embrace the great Eternal all,
  No more the Holy Spirit grieve,

Go preach Baptism in Christ's name!
For this Commandment He has given;
The Saviour once from glory came,
And marked the road, the way to Heaven.

HYMN 169.

Should Hell oppose and Satan rage,
And all my inward powers engage;
Oh, Christ! my Lord! come take my part,
And bind to Thee my wandering heart.

Should we in sin and darkness live,
How could that Holy God forgive?
If we pray with fervent heart,
He will His grace to us impart.

Could I avoid the tempter's rage,
And in my Maker's cause engage,
My heart and tongue with fervent zeal,
His loving kindness hope to feel.

Sin, the source of heartfelt sorrow,
The cause of grief and pain to-morrow
Oh, cleanse my soul from sin and shame,
Teach us to love and fear Thy name.

HYMN 170.

Behold the Lamb that once was slain,
In awful grandeur in the skies ;
We'll shout and sing to His dear name,
With joyful songs our voices raise.

Behold how Christ the Saviour died,
To pay the debt that sin hath made ;
The Jews, they mocked, their God denied,
While He their dreadful ransom paid.

Behold Him bleeding on the tree,
For such poor sinful souls as mine ;
The Earth it quaked from sea to sea,
The dazzling sun refused to shine.

HYMN 171.

Sinners, come hear Thy Saviour's voice,
  And see the Cross, the Crown He wore;
Repent! believe! with Saints rejoice,
  And view His dreadful sufferings o'er.

Come, sinners! come! and don't refuse,
  But hear that grand, inviting voice;
Salvation! oh, that joyful news!
  It makes both Heaven and Earth rejoice.

Oh, could we climb that joyful road,
  There view the glories of the place,
We could not sin against our God,
  Or trample on His boundless grace.

Sin is the cause of all our woes,
  For sin the Cross our Saviour bore;
Our grief and sorrow here He knows,
  His flesh had felt them long before.

HYMN 172.

Oh, Lord of Heaven, of power and love!
  We fain would see Thy sacred face,
In Glory there, in Heaven above,
  And sing the riches of Thy Grace.

Religion! oh, that gift from God,
  His church, his Holy Sabbath day,
The sacred pages of His Word;
  We must arise without delay.

Arise! embrace the living God!
  He will His love, His grace impart;
Show us the path Christ Jesus trod,
  And write His precepts on our heart.

May we Thy great Salvation feel,
  And try to make that better choice;
Fulfil Thy law with Holy zeal,
  And hear Thy kind inviting voice.

HYMN 173.

That awful day will soon be here,
  When man must meet his final doom;
His Judge in Glory will appear,
  How dreadful must the summons come.

That awful day of dark despair
  To those who never knew the Lord;
Will Thou, oh, God! my soul prepare,
  Through faith in Thine Eternal Word.

Great God, forbear! be pleased to hear
  A prayer, through Christ, to Thee in
      Heaven;
Soothe our minds, dispel our fear,
  And speak the word our sins forgiven.

Protect us in that awful hour,
  Whem Time itself shall fade away;
And guard us with Thy sovereign power,
  To fairer worlds and brighter day.

HYMN 174.

Firm as a rock Thy Word endures,
  If Heaven and Earth should pass away;
While all we need, Thy Hand procures,
  And guards us safe from day to day.

Firm as Thy Throne Thy promise stands,
  To those who do their Maker's will,
Their eyes shall see those Holy lands,
  Their feet shall walk to Zion's Hill.

Firm as the Earth Thy Gospel Grace,
  To those who trust Thine only Son;
They shall behold that happy place,
  And say, with joy, "Thy will be done!"

Then, oh, my soul! march boldly on;
  Pursue that heavenly, happy way,
To Heaven, where Christ my Saviour's gone,
  Where all is one eternal day.

HYMN 175.

Christ, the head, the corner-stone,
  Whereon my hope of Heaven depends ;
He trod the wine-press here alone,
  To meet those great eternal ends.

Christ, the head, the corner-stone,
  The stone the builders did refuse ;
Yet He will bless and save His own,
  The Greeks, the Gentiles, or the Jews.

Christ, the head, the corner-stone,
  He bears my sinking spirits up ;
He blessed and claimed us for His own ;
  How can we sink with such a prop ?

Christ, the head, the corner-stone,
  Whereon the Church of God is built ;
He fought the fight, the victory won,
  Redeemed the world from sin and guilt.

Christ, the head, the corner-stone,
  A shadowing rock in a weary land;
His grace and kindness have made known,
  And placed the meek at His right hand.

Christ, the head, the corner-stone,
  He left His Father's realms above;
His great commission here made known,
  When moved by pity and by love.

Christ, the head, the corner-stone,
  The Christian's guide to glory bright;
Salvation comes through Him alone;
  The contrite soul is His delight.

HYMN 176.

A Call to the Sinner.

Oh, careless sinner! come!
  Pray, now attend!
This world is not your home;
  It soon will end.

Your Saviour calls aloud;
Do not delay!
Forsake the thoughtless crowd;
Christ is the way.

No hope of joy to find,
While thus you go;
No peace unto your mind,
But sin and woe.

Alas! why will ye slight,
And still refuse
The rays of Gospel light,
And darkness choose?

Come, make your choice to-day,
And be at rest;
And try the good old way,
That Christ has blest!

HYMN 177.

Salvation! oh, thy healing streams!
With joy I view thy radiant beams,
And hope, through Christ, to be at rest,
And reign with Him among the blest.

Religious joys, that heavenly prize,
May nothing short my soul suffice;
I hope, through faith and humble prayer,
To wash away the stains I wear.

Oh, could mine eyes yet live to see
Thy heralds crowned with victory;
The heathen come and learn to pray,
And cast their Idol Gods away;

And trust the great, the true Messiah,
Their hearts be filled with pure desire;
To bow before His Throne of Grace,
And plead their dark, benighted case.

HYMN 178.

Sin doth destroy our feeble race,
 And leads to death and dark despair;
It spoils and blasts the comely face,
 And tells of bliss we know not where.

Sin, Hell and Satan all unite,
 To mar our peace and joys in life;
Our fell destroyer's chief delight,
 To dwell in sin and wicked strife.

The seeds of sin, by Adam sown,
 Are evil snares and foul deceit;
Before the Gospel was made known,
 We had no guide to guard our feet.

Sin, the source of fear and grief,
 The vital cause of all our pain;
Oh, send Thy balm, that gives relief!
 Restore us to Thy joys again!

HYMN 179.

How could I longer hold my peace,
  While I can raise my feeble voice?
My thoughts and views so much increase,
  It makes my heart and soul rejoice.

Oh, could I feel Thy sovereign grace,
  And know my Saviour's love and care,
In Heaven to bow before Thy face,
  With leave to claim my mansion there!

Then would my raptured spirit sing
  Before Jehovah's mighty throne,
And make those Courts of Glory ring
  With songs to me before unknown.

HYMN 180.

When I survey Thy glories, Lord,
And read the pages of Thy Word,
My inward powers and soul would say,
Can I appear at Judgment Day ?

When I survey Thy boundless grace,
And view myself before Thy face,
These thoughts then bear a dreadful sway :
I must appear at Judgment Day !

When I survey the Heavens above,
There view my Maker, clothed in love,
And hear the Lord in glory say :
"Prepare thyself for Judgment Day !"

When I survey the world around,
And view myself to Judgment bound,
My former life then I survey,
And feel the pangs of Judgment Day !

When I survey Christ's wounded side,
The cruel Cross whereon He died,
Methinks I hear him kindly say:
"You shall be spared at Judgment Day!"

Oh, may my soul with holy zeal
These kind emotions ever feel;
And at that last and final day,
On Angels' wings be borne away!

HYMN 181.

On Canaan's land, that happy place,
I have a pure, a firm desire,
To see my Maker's throne of grace,
And there His glories to admire.

Jerusalem, the Christian's home,
Oft would I wish to be
In that abode, no more to roam,
In sweet humility.

That glorious place of perfect bliss,
  That shore I hope to make ;
Oh, God of Mercy, grant me this,
  Forgive, for Jesus's sake.

That bright abode where Jesus reigns,
  I hope one day to see,
And sing His love in sweeter strains,
  Through all Eternity.

HYMN 182.

When I survey God's mighty throne,
  And view the Lamb for sinner's slain,
To make the Gospel tidings known,
  Christ suffered death in Gethsemane.

The true Messiah, the great High Priest,
  By prophets long foretold to be,
The Gospel light, that living feast,
  Old Simeon cried, I have lived to see.

That gloomy garden long will be
   A place so awful and sublime;
The cruel Cross, that woful tree,
   Where Christ, our Saviour, did resign.

There did resign and died for all
   Who may His loving kindness choose;
Who on His Sacred name may call,
   His tender mercies won't refuse.

HYMN 183.

Religion! oh, that Heavenly truth—
   It bears the sinking sinner up;
It comforts age, a guide to youth,
   And sweetens every bitter cup.

Religion! what a glorious theme!
   The vital spark to life divine;
Our troubles here pass like a dream,
   When we our hearts to God resign.

Religion ! oh, thy healing streams,
The carnal mind can't never view ;
Christ's love through all its radiant beams,
The false Apostate never knew.

Religion ! thy transcendent joys,
God's love and grace to me impart ;
Oh, raise my mind from Earthly toys,
And bind to Thee my wandering heart.

HYMN 184.

Great is the Lord ! all creatures say,
And all His mandates must prevail ;
The Heavens and Earth shall pass away,
Before Jehovah's word can fail.

Great is the Lord ! before whose face
Nations must bow, their homage pay,
And plead for His protecting grace,
To save them in that fearful day.

Great is the Lord ! before whose throne
  Saints and Sinners must appear,
And there to stand or fall alone,
  Their solemn sentence then to hear.

Great is the Lord ! before whose voice
  The planets in awful grandeur move,
And Angels bow, the Heavens rejoice,
  Before His majesty and love.

HYMN 185.

Clothed in love, with power supreme,
  The mighty Saviour did appear ;
Salvation was his only theme,
  His great, His glorious mission here.

He left His Father's Courts on High,
  The soul of man lay near his heart ;
Came down to Earth to bleed and die,
  Then joys immortal did impart.

Here Christ, the Gospel light, appeared;
  The Saints the joyful news proclaimed;
Through Christ, the sinner's heart was cheered,
  To sing the glories of His name.

The true Messiah, our great High Priest,
  Clothed in light, from Heaven He came;
He invites us to a richer feast,
  The marriage supper of the Lamb.

HYMN 186 — Baptism.

Our great High Priest to Heaven is gone,
  In Jordan's stream baptized by John;
He left the great example here,
  To all when duty may appear.

Baptism rites he did ordain,
  Through which, a blessing we obtain;
The kind example he has given,
  A guide, a way-mark home, to Heaven.

He was immersed in Jordan's wave,
 There did descend a watery grave ;
There from the deep He gently rose,
 And mildly conquered all His foes.

In Jordan's wave He gently bowed,
 The water was His closing shroud ;
His mandates here we must obey,
 To meet Him in the coming day.

HYMN 187.

Behold ! how Christ, our Saviour pleads
 In Heaven, His Father to forbear :
The great Immanuel intercedes
 With God, our sinful souls to spare.

While clothed with majesty and light,
 He hears the vilest sinner call ;
The contrite soul is His delight,
 His grace is free to one and all.

He endured the Cross, He wore the Crown,
 He died a hard and cruel death ;

From Heaven He brought Salvation down,
And sealed it with His dying breath.

In anguish there our Saviour prayed—
"Father, oh may this cup depart,
Yet, nevertheless, Thy will," He said,
"Without a murmur from my heart."

HYMN 188.

Christ, our Lord, the great Messiah,
Now dwells above at God's right hand;
Give me that faith, that pure desire,
Through prayer to see that Holy land.

The sinner's friend, Thou God of Host,
Oh, keep me safe from sin and harm;
Baptize me with the Holy Ghost,
Protect me with Thy mighty arm.

Thy sovereign power, Thy searching eye,
Before Thy throne I would appear;
Teach me the road to Thee on high,
Subdue my sin and slavish fear.

Teach me to walk that righteous way,
  Subdue my carnal mind to Thee—
To bear my Cross from day to day,
  At last Thy great Salvation see.

HYMN 189.

Poor sinful souls of Adam's race,
  Who have no sure abiding place,
Come taste the joys of life divine,
  Thy wicked hearts to God resign.

Come plead thy dark, benighted case
  Before thy Maker's Throne of Grace,
And pray to Him to be forgiven—
  Prepare Thy soul to reign in Heaven.

Come, Sinner! don't no more delay,
  But try the straight and narrow way
That leads to life in yonder sky—
  Embrace the Lord, why will ye die?

Oh! Sinner, turn! embrace the truth,
  From hoary heads to careless youth,

And cleave to Christ, Thy Sovereign Lord,
  And Heaven shall be Thy sure reward.

HYMN 190.

A precious hope through Christ is given,
  Though dead in sin I yet may live
And find my way by prayer to Heaven,
  If I repent, He will forgive.

The contrite soul God will forgive,
  By grace and mercy He is known ;
Lay hold of strength, we yet may live,
  I'll place my trust in Him alone.

How could my heart so long refuse
  Thy Holy doctrine so divine?
Thy love and mercy so abuse !
  Oh, cleanse this wicked soul of mine.

Direct me through life's journey here,
  Evil and few my days at most :
When death shall seal the parting tear,
  Then land me on fair Canaan's coast.

HYMN 191.

When heart and strength and life shall fail,
  Oh, what a sad and mournful tale
To see a sinner pressed with years,
  Laden with guilt and slavish fears.

His hoary locks bespoke his age,
  His garb was like an ancient sage,
His quivering limbs a tale of woe,
  Down to the grave he soon must go.

Oh, could he say "God's will, Amen,
  I've lived my years three score and ten;
My feeble frame I now resign—
  Oh, save this sinking soul of mine."

But onward still this sinner goes,
  Prèssed with years and heavy woes,
Down to the grave in dark despair,
  No hope of mercy enters there.

Ah, what a bright and pleasing tale,
  When heart and strength and life shall fail,

To hear a dying saint reply—
" 'Tis meet that I was born to die."

HYMN 192. Gospel Light.

Let vile apostates rage and say—
"Religious joys are idle dreams;"
The world can't give or take away
The Gospel light, its radiant beams.

While sinful man pursues his way
To the dark realms of endless night,
Feed me, oh Lord, from day to day,
With balmy dews of Gospel light.

Let poor backsliders scoff and jeer,
Let Satan rage and vent his spite;
Teach me Thy law, Thy love and fear,
The riches of Thy Gospel light.

Let Satan all his powers employ,
To spoil my peace, destroy my sight;
Show me the path to endless joy,
Thy boundless grace and Gospel light.

HYMN 193.

Great is Thy power, Almighty God,
  Thy judgment bar—oh, how august!
We fear the vengeance of Thy rod,
  But still in Thee, I'll place my trust.

Oh, God! convert my soul to Thee,
  Thy mighty arm is clothed in love;
Let me Thy courts, Thy glory see,
  And sing Thy praise in realms above.

Sin, my worst enemy while here,
  No more will mar or spoil my peace;
Before Thy face I shall appear—
  Then will my woes and sorrows cease.

There angels bow before Thy throne,
  With loud Hosannas shout Amen,
With praises to the Eternal Son,
  Crying "Worthy, worthy is the Lamb."

HYMN 194.

Prayer, a strong and mighty tower,
A chariot to the worlds above;
It prepares us for a dying hour,
Secures the pledge of Jesus's love.

Prayer, like an anchor to the soul,
It calms the surging waves of life—
It makes our moments sweetly roll,
Destroys contention, sin and strife.

Prayer is the Christian's vital breath,
It binds the weak and broken heart;
It soothes us on the bed of death,
And Heavenly blessings doth impart.

The praying soul is not dismayed,
This path the dying martyrs trod;
The Saviour oft in secret prayed,
And held communion with His God.

Prayer, the only path to Heaven,
The path the great Apostles trod;
The kind examples Christ has given,
Whereby we intercede with God.

Christ often to His Father prayed,
In mountains wild, in humble strains;
While on the Cross was not dismayed,
When life poured from His bleeding veins.

HYMN 195.

I would to God that I had been
A Christian all my days:
Despised the wicked paths of sin,
And walked in wisdom's ways.

But oh, alas! that has not been,
I've wandered from the Lord
With heartfelt sorrow now and then,
While reading in His Word.

I hope through Christ and humble prayer,
My sins may be forgiven,
And see His great Salvation there,
And praise my God in Heaven.

But when I view His blessings o'er,
And view my sin and wicked ways,

His Holy name I would adore,
  In joyful hopes of brighter days.

HYMN 196.

Hail ! Thou glorious, mighty being,
  Who left Thy Father's realms above ;
Came down to Earth, our misery seeing,
  Clothed with holiness and love.

Hail ! Thou wondrous, mighty Saviour,
  Lord of Light and Prince of Peace—
Who suffered shame for our behavior,
  Our joys or woes through Him will cease.

Should we embrace our great Salvation,
  Whereon our hopes of Heaven depend,
And mind the truths of Revelation,
  Then will our troubles have an end.

Should we neglect this great Salvation,
  Until our days are finished here :
Then at that awful retribution,
  How will our mortal soul appear ?

HYMN 197. The Pilgrim.

Am I a pilgrim here below—
  A servant of the Lord?
One thing I wish to learn and know,
  The riches of His Word.

Am I a pilgrim here below—
  A follower of the Lamb?
May I His grace and goodness know,
  And learn to praise His name.

Am I a pilgrim here below—
  And bound to heathen lands?
I wish His Holy will to know,
  And keep His great commands.

Am I a pilgrim here below—
  A traveler to afar?
Do I love the Lord, or no—
  The bright and Morning Star?

HYMN 198.

If we should to the end endure,
  A Crown of Glory we shall gain;
This God hath spoke His promise sure,
  None ever found His service vain.

But should we faint and turn aside,
  And all His warnings disobey,
We must expect to be denied,
  By Him in that great trying day.

But if we gain that dazzling Crown,
  A glittering robe of white,
With Martyrs, Prophets, then sit down,
  In scenes of pure delight.

Our cup is full, our souls would say;
  We ask for nothing more;
There sing God's praise from day to day,
  On that celestial shore.

HYMN 199. On Baptism.

A glorious way-mark Christ has given ;
He was immersed in Jordan's wave,
To guide the Christian home to Heaven,
Yet this alone can never save.

We must repent and be baptized,
And read His Holy Word with care ;
For He Himself was sacrificed,
That we might find admission there.

Baptism rites Christ did ordain,
To guide us on that heavenly road,
And made the duty clear and plain,
The path is straight to His abode.

Says Christ : " These rites I now ordain ;
Ye must repent and trust my Word ;
And then thy soul in joy shall reign,
With Christ, thy Friend and Sovereign
Lord.

HYMN 200.

Am I a Soldier of the Cross,
  A servant of that Mighty King?
My treasures here I'll count but dross,
  And of His great salvation sing.

Am I a servant of the Lord,
  An heir of Heaven at His Right Hand?
Then I must read His Holy Word,
  With hopes to see that happy land.

My soul in raptures then would be,
  To view the Father on His Throne;
The fullness of the Godhead see,
  The Holy Ghost, the Mighty Son.

How can my soul in sin remain,
  While Heavenly bliss appears in view?
He shows the way, and makes it plain;
  His Holy footsteps then pursue.

HYMN 201.

While I survey God's powerful hand,
  And think how weak and frail I be;
While worlds revolve at His command,
  That great first cause I hope to see.

Through prayer and faith, His glory see,
  In that abode of heavenly bliss;
Through boundless ages there to be;
  Oh, God of Mercy! grant me this.

Oh, Lord! how could I be denied?
  Grant me that boon, Thy love and grace;
To think how Christ for sinners died,
  Let me behold His sacred face.

Thus while I view with heart-felt joy,
  Show me a mansion for mine own
Let Earth and Hell no more decoy,
  But let me praise Thee round Thy throne.

May I resolve with all my heart,
  With soul and mind, to serve the Lord,

And pledge my all to not depart,
  But rest securely on Thy Word.

HYMN 202. The Resurrection.

Christ on the Cross for us was slain,
  While there for man the ransom paid,
He tasted death, then rose again,
  While in the tomb His body laid.

There in the tomb our Saviour laid,
  While guards of soldiers round Him set,
The tomb that was by Joseph made,
  With massive stones the door was shut.

His resurrection soon appeared;
  Bright Angels rolled the stones away;
The Jews, his keepers, shook and feared,
  While Christ arose and went His way.

"All hail!" the son of God did say,
  When first to Mary He appeared;
That hallowed morn, that holy day,
  By Gospel light the world was cheered.

" Be not afraid !" our Saviour saith,
  " Go, tell my brethren I have risen ;
I 've spoiled the foe, the monster death,
  And burst the tomb, that gloomy prison."

HYMN 203.

Repent, vain man ! and be baptized,
  And come while yet there is room ;
" Give ear to me !" the Saviour cries,
  " Lest death may seal thy doom."

" Repent !" the God of Justice cries ;
  " While time and space are given ;
In Jordan's waters be baptized,
  And shape thy course for Heaven."

" Repent !" thy Great Redeemer cries ;
  " Have faith, believe and live !"
Trust in the Lord and be baptized ;
  He will our sins forgive.

" Repent !" the Voice of Mercy cries,
  And all the Heavenly Host ;

May we with water be baptized,
And with the Holy Ghost.

HYMN 204.

Let not a lie escape your tongue,
But keep your conscience clear;
And never think yourself too young
The God of Hosts to fear.

Let not a lie escape your tongue,
But keep your garments pure;
These words concern the old or young;
Who can a lie endure?

Who can endure a wicked lie,
And in that sin remain?
Remember this, that we must die,
And meet them all again.

Let not a lie your lips escape,
But mind and speak the truth;
Avoid that sin in every shape,
While in the paths of youth.

HYMN 205.

Job was a servant of the Lord;
He kept His counsels, feared His Word,
And when he felt His chastening rod,
His lips sinned not against his God.

Then let us Job's example mind,
Then grace and mercy we shall find;
Then at that last and trying hour,
God will guard us with His power.

This way the old Apostles tried;
They bore their cross, subdued their pride,
And bowed before the Lamb of God,
And walked the path our Saviour trod.

At death they meet that shining host,
The Father, Son, and Holy Ghost;
And view the Godhead there above,
Clothed in a robe of light and love.

HYMN 206.

Sure is Thy Throne and great reward,
  And all Thy heavenly blessings sure,
To those who trust Thy Holy Word,
  And to the end endure.

Lord, may Thy grace, like summer's sun,
  Warm this cold heart of mine ;
I would that race of glory run,
  A journey so divine.

Teach me Thy boundless grace and love,
  And seal my wandering heart
To Thy blessed courts in worlds above,
  There never more to part.

Thus while with melting heart I view
  My Saviour's dying love,
Oh, when I bid this Earth adieu,
  Take me to realms above.

HYMN 207.

Come, Sinner! hear thy Saviour's voice!
  Why will you more delay?
Lay hold of strength, make Him your choice,
  And choose the better way.

How can you stand and hear Him call,
  And feel no inward fear?
For Death's cold hand would spoil it all;
  How then will you appear?

While you have health, and strength and power,
  With time and space to do,
Prepare to meet a dying hour,
  And flee from sin and woe.

King Jesus on His dazzling throne,
  He calls on you to come;
Your wants and troubles there make known;
  Come, enter! there is room.

With smiles and love, he cries, "Give ear!
The haughty, vain, and proud,
Prepare yourselves for glory here,
To meet me in the clouds."

HYMN 208.

If I were called to preach His Word,
To bear a message from the Lord,
One thing I could not be denied,
To preach a Saviour crucified.

Then I should glory in the Cross,
And count my treasures here but dross;
To spend my breath in Heathen lands,
And try to do His great commands.

His great commission I would bear,
And preach a dying Saviour there;
And warn the nations far and near,
Their Great Redeemer's name to fear.

There I would preach and spend my breath,
And when my voice is lost in death,

On Angels' wings to Heaven be borne,
Leave friends and brethren here to mourn.

HYMN 209.

Mysterious are Thy ways, oh God!
Thy works to man past finding out;
Yet we may read and trust Thy Word,
To pray and nothing doubt.

Jehovah! give us faith in Thee;
Teach us how to pray aright;
May we Thy humble followers be,
For such is Thy delight.

Come, Holy Spirit! cheer my heart,
With Thy enlivening power;
Let me from Thee no more depart,
With joy I'll hail each hour.

With joy I'll hail the blessed day,
When my Redeemer came,
When down to Earth He made His way;
Hosanna to his name!

HYMN 210.

While in this tenement of clay,
Lord, teach me how to live!
Learn me to watch as well as pray,
And all my sins forgive.

Show me the way that leads to Heaven,
The path that Moses trod;
And kindly speak my sins forgiven;
Oh, Thou, that Holy God!

To Thee we raise our wishful eyes,
And ask Thy boundless grace;
May nothing short our souls suffice,
But love in Thine embrace.

We should embrace Thy Holy Word,
And claim Thy promise sure;
Have faith in our ascended Lord,
Like soldiers then endure.

HYMN 211.

Hosanna to the Almighty God,
  Who bids the planets roll;
We fear and tremble at His Word,
  His sceptre sways the whole.

His power, His goodness and His grace,
  Being all combined in one;
Could I but see that Sacred face,
  That high and Holy One.

This powerful God is ours,
  Our Father and our King;
He guards us with His Heavenly powers,
  And teaches us to sing.

How dare we longer still refuse
  To hear His mighty voice?
The road to death and darkness choose,
  Oh, what a wretched choice!

HYMN 212.

Thine is the power, oh God of Light,
  Thine is the praise and glory, too;
Teach us to read and pray aright,
  Thy Holy will with faith to do.

Thy Heavenly doctrine, pure, divine,
  Shall be my chief and sole delight—
Cheer this benighted heart of mine
  With Thy pure, transcendent light.

Give us Thy glorious Gospel light,
  A lamp to guide to brighter day :
There see the Saints in robes of white,
  Through trials sore have made their way.

Their glittering robes in glory shine,
  Their dazzling crowns like rays of light,
Oh, could such Heavenly bliss be mine,
  With Christ, my Lord, in glory bright.

HYMN 213.

Great is the Lord, His power is great,
  And all His attributes are just;
The Heavenly Host His mandates wait,
  In Him I hope to place my trust.

Trust in that wise, unerring God,
  Who rules the Universe below;
His arm that wields that awful rod,
  Hath power to strike or spare the blow.

Direct my will and guard my frame
  To keep Thy precepts and Thy laws;
To learn to praise Thy Holy name,
  Thou God of love, the great first cause.

Help me to make that wiser choice,
  To flee from sin and turn to Thee;
To hear Thy pure and Heavenly voice,
  Prepare with joy Thy courts to see.

HYMN 214.

Our Saviour's love, so great, so pure,
He left His Father's courts on high;
For man, the Cross He did endure,
On Calvary's mount did bleed and die.

He endured the Cross, despised the shame,
Redeemed the World from sin and guilt,
He glorified His Father's name,
There His atoning blood was spilt.

There on the Cross for sinners prayed,
Besought His Father to forgive;
"They know not what they do," He said,
"Let them return to Thee and live."

His great commission here He bore,
That Holy law He satisfied;
He has gone to Heaven forevermore,
And left the record how He died.

His dying pangs, His parting groans,
Made the Earth with terrors quake;

The face of nature seemed to mourn,
The flinty rocks asunder brake.

Then gloom and horror spread around,
The sun refused its rays of light;
Convulsive shocks then shook the ground,
What a sad, an awful sight.

"It's finished, now," the Saviour cried,
When to His Father He had prayed;
He bowed His gentle head and died—
The Jews around Him stood dismayed.

HYMN 215.

The Pilgrim's Journey.

Dark and sandy, wild the desert,
Where the pilgrim marches through;
Yet, beyond those scenes of sorrow,
He finds his treasures bright and new.

Yet, mighty is his great commander,
Bids him cross and never fear;

'Mid Satan's rage and all his slander,
  The Saviour doth his spirit cheer.

Satan's force shall not defeat thee,
  Bend thy course for Canaan's shore;
Should the river Jordan meet thee,
  Christ has entered that before.

Pilgrim, see those scenes before thee,
  Satan raging at his loss;
Should the powers of Hell surround thee,
  Sing the triumphs of the Cross.

HYMN 216.

Come! sinner, hear! and don't forbear,
  Thy Saviour's kind, inviting voice;
For Heavenly bliss thy soul prepare,
  And with that shining host rejoice.

Come! sinner, come! no more delay,
  And let thy sin and folly cease;
Prepare thyself for judgment day,
  Thy soul to see the land of peace.

Oh, Lord, wilt Thou my sins forgive,
  Let me escape Thy wrath to come ;
A Godly life pray let me live,
  And claim Thy promise as my own.

To claim that promise firm and sure,
  And bear my Cross while here below—
And try to keep my garments pure,
  At death to scenes of glory go.

HYMN 217.

Jerusalem, that Heavenly place,
  Where all the Saints and Angels dwell ;
They dwell before their Maker's face,
  No finite soul their joys can tell.

Jerusalem, that land of love,
  The place where my Redeemer reigns ;
Had I the pinions of a dove,
  To rise and see those Heavenly plains.

But oh, alas ! my sinful soul
  Must cleave to Christ to be forgiven ;

May He my inward powers control,
  And raise my feeble thoughts to Heaven.

Should hell and sin their powers unite,
  And try to lead my feet astray;
Give me Thy grace, Thy Gospel light,
  That leads to one eternal day.

HYMN 218.

Thou great first cause of power and might,
  Who bids the Earth in grandeur move;
Who made the Sun, that orb of light,
  Yet still Thine arm is clothed in love.

Thy power is awful and sublime,
  No flesh can stand before Thy face;
Thy voice would cause the end of time,
  Yet Thou hast built a throne of grace.

But when I view Thy powerful hand,
  And of Thy Heavenly wonders think:
How worlds revolve at Thy command,
  Oh, into nothing then I shrink.

Yet, when I view Thy love and care,
And think of Christ's atoning blood,
Direct my feet and guide me there—
Teach me to know that Thou art God.

HYMN 219.

One thing, oh God, pray let me learn,
Thus while my lamp holds out to burn,
To keep Thy precepts and Thy laws,
And worship Thee, Thou great first cause.

Before the cold and silent grave
Shall bury master and his slave,
And all be levelled to the Earth,
That land that gave to each their birth.

Then when the spark of life is fled,
And all its beating pulse are dead;
If I have trusted in the Lord,
Then Heaven will be my great reward.

Then when in death's cold, icy shade,
Honor, power, and fame are laid—
And every creature's place is given,
Pray let me come to Thee in Heaven.

HYMN 220.

Oh! Jesus, our Saviour, Thy love and good will,
Should prompt human nature Thy law to fulfil:
To think of Thy sufferings, Thy sorrow and pain,
How can we deny Thee or trespass again?

In the day of Salvation now let us prepare,
And place ourselves under His kindness and care;
In sweet meditation through faith I can see
My Saviour in glory now pleading for me.

With love and compassion, saying, "Father, forbear!

Their souls I have ransomed, I pray Thee
to spare;
Oh, send Thy conviction their hearts to control,—
In their great tribulation remember their
souls."

While Satan is trying our peace to destroy,
With art and persuasion, with lies to decoy,
Thy love, grace and mercy, our only restraint,
Look down from bright glory and hear our
complaint.

From the regions of glory wilt Thou condescend
To hear our petition, our God and our
friend,
To guard us and keep us with mercy and
power,
In the midst of affliction to solace the hour.

In the mansions of glory our Saviour doth
dwell,
Who died to redeem us and save us from
hell;

May His grace and His goodness, His mercy and love,
At death then remove us to regions above:

Where myriads of Angels and Saints do adore
The Father of Mercy when time is no more—
A shouting Hosanna to the Father and Son,
Even so let it be—Hallelujah! Amen!

HYMN 221.—Rev. 22d Chap.

The Waters and Tree of Life.

There an Angel of glory appeared to his view,
And showed to St. John the waters of life,
And told him these sayings were faithful and true,
The reward of the righteous is eternal life.

There out of God's throne the waters proceed,
In the midst of the streets a tree there is found:

Its leaves and its fruits supply all their need,
A cure for the sick, a balm for a wound.

In the midst of that city God's glory doth shine,
There Jesus, our Saviour, and Angels of light,
How oft would I wish those glories were mine,
The Day-Star has risen and never comes night.

There He said unto John, "Be faithful and true!
Behold! I come quickly, and blessed is he;
My grace is sufficient for Gentile or Jew—
To all true believers this city is free."

That mansion of rest, that Heaven above,
Free from all trouble, from sorrow and care,
Our Saviour to see in His glory and love,
That beautiful tree of life growing there.

He that is righteous must be righteous still,
And he that is filthy will filthy remain;

Then let us be humble and try to fulfil,
A crown of bright glory we all shall obtain.

Behold! I come quickly, and bring my reward
To those who prove faithful, on Jesus depend:
For He is our Saviour, our King and our Lord,
Alpha and Omega, beginning and end.

HYMN 222. On Baptism.

Baptism, oh, that Sacred rite,
Bequeathed to us by Christ above,
What joy it gives, what pure delight,
When we obey in faith and love.

When to the water's side we go,
With hearts sincere and motives pure,
What streams of endless pleasures flow
To those who to the end endure.

To imitate our blessed Lord,
  And be immersed in Jordan's wave,
Christ's church to join in sweet accord,
  With hopes of life beyond the grave.

"Repent!" says Christ, "and be baptized,
  This sacred rite I freely give;
Since I for thee was sacrificed,
  Take up thy Cross through faith and live.

HYMN 223.

Oh for a hope in Thee, my God,
  That happy frame of mind,
To walk the path that Moses trod,
  Thy endless joys to find.

Oh for a hope in Christ, Thy Son,
  To feel my sins forgiven;
That race of joy and glory run,
  Then dwell with Thee in Heaven.

Oh for a hope beyond the grave,
  Which gold or wealth can't buy;
Pray condescend our souls to save—
  Lord, hear our feeble cry.

Oh for a hope to reign on high,
  And hear those harps of gold—
Where streams of pleasure never dry,
  Thy glorious face behold.

HYMN 224.

Straight is the path that leads to life,
  Annoyed by folly, sin and strife;
Broad is the road that leads to death,
  So the blessed Gospel saith.

But straight and narrow is the way
  That leads to life and endless day;
To do God's will and travel there,
  Be that my aim and daily prayer.

And when I pray with fervent heart,
  Christ, my Saviour, takes my part;

Should Satan rage and Hell unite,
  Our God will save His heart's delight.

When Christ shall come to judge the world,
  And time is to destruction hurled;
Oh God, be my Eternal friend,
  And take me home when life shall end.

HYMN 225.

Father, to Thee mine eyes I raise,
  And pray for Thy forgiving grace:
To shout and sing through endless days,
  In joy supreme before Thy face.

I ask these favors, God of Light,
  Through no merits of my own,
But may I ever keep in sight
  The death and sufferings of Thy Son.

No worth or worthiness in me,
  No claim to Thy protecting care;
Through Jesus Christ I hope to see
  Thy gracious face and glories there.

To see the Lamb that once was slain,
  And bow before His mercy-seat:
In glory there forever reign,
  And all our friends and kindred meet.

HYMN 226. Acts, Chap. 8.

Philip Baptizeth the Eunuch.

"Here is water," to the Eunuch cried,
  Then stopped his chariot wheels—
And then descended to the tide,
  What inward joys he feels.

"If ye believe," then Philip cries,
  "With all thine heart, ye may
Now in the water be baptized,
  Here on this blessed day."

"I do believe," the Ethiop said,
  "Christ is the Son of God;
I'll bear my Cross—be not afraid
  To sound His name abroad."

Down to the waters they did go,
  This humble man obeyed;
Christ's great example here below,
  On whom his heart was stayed.

Now justified the Eunuch feels,
  While Philip disappeared;
He urges on his chariot wheels,
  His anxious heart was cheered.

HYMN 227.

If we to God in meekness come,
  He never will deny—
But take us to that Heavenly home,
  Where pleasures never die.

To take us to His blest abode,
  His great Salvation know;
There to behold our Maker, God,
  Where joys celestial flow.

To view the Heavens with vast delight,
  Bright shining as the Sun,

Secure from sin and endless night,
  Our race to glory run.

With raptured spirits there to sing
  In songs of sweeter strains
Before our Universal King,
  And view those gorgeous plains.

HYMN 228.

Youth's golden hours will soon be gone,
  Should life but lose the vital spark,
Their morning sun may set at noon,
  And ever leave them in the dark.

Youth's rosy cheek and sparkling eye
  Turns pale and dim at every hour;
We mortals bloom, then fade and die,
  God governs all with Sovereign power.

Youth, like the Spring, will pass away,
  And all its beating pulse be dead;
But oh! that last, that final day
  Breaks o'er my soul with solemn dread.

Youth's active limbs and glittering joys,
  Would almost promise things divine ;
But Time, our health, our strength destroys,
  And steals away this life of mine.

HYMN 229.

It is true that Salvation is offered to-day,
  As to Predestination, no mortal can say ;
The tenets of doctrines, I leave them behind,
  The laws of my Saviour and precepts to mind.

All one in Christ Jesus, who walk in the faith,
  Who in union agree, the Evangelist saith ;
Persuasions in Heaven there never can be,
  The Saints there in glory in union agree.

Let no wild dissension of doctrine possess,
  But before all the world our Saviour confess ;
The plan of Jehovah is loving and kind,
  The system was formed by an unerring mind.

All names and persuasions are nothing to me,
  If I can the mansions of happiness see ;

To dwell with my Saviour Eternity round,
And sing Hallelujah on that happy ground.

HYMN 230.

When death shall end our journey here,
And blast the comely face,
And friends shall drop the parting tear,
Lord, save us with Thy grace!

When we shall leave this Earth below,
And quit this house of clay,
May we to God in glory go,
Through one Eternal Day!

When we shall quit this feeble frame,
Our pulse all cease to beat,
May we sing praises to His name,
And sit at Jesus's feet!

When all our sins are done away,
Our pilgrimage is o'er,
To sing through one Eternal Day,
On that celestial shore!

HYMN 231. On Prayer.

Prayer, the Christian's path to Heaven,
The path our loving Saviour trod;
He prayed that we might be forgiven,
And dwell before that holy God.

Prayer drives the Tempter far away,
It bears the soul in trials up;
It guards from sin each fleeting day,
And soothes to us each bitter cup.

I would that I might always pray,
And tell my Saviour all my grief;
And keep the straight and narrow way;
Then he will send my soul relief.

I think how oft our Saviour prayed,
When sins of millions bore him down;
"Father! teach them," there he said,
"To pray in faith to gain a crown."

HYMN 232.

Oh God, why are we so depraved,
So prone to folly, sin and guilt?
It's through Thy Son mankind are saved,
For on the Cross His blood was spilt.

Why are our feet so prone to stray,
To leave the paths of truth and light,
To walk that broad and sinful way,
Down to the shades of endless night?

Down to the regions of despair,
Where all is dark, and vapors roll;
No hope of mercy enters there,
To save the dying, sinking soul.

God grant that this may never be!
Arrest us in our wild career;
Direct our minds and will to Thee;
Wilt Thou our great petition hear?

HYMN 233.

The Preacher's Desire.

Oh, Lord! if I am called to preach,
  Thy holy doctrines may I teach;
Help me to draw the lines of truth,
  To age, to middle age, and youth.

Thy great commission I would bear,
  Thy Gospel truths in faith declare;
To preach Salvation through Thy Son,
  Until my Gospel work is done.

I 'll take my counsel from Thy Word,
  And preach of my ascended Lord,
And while I live on Earth to preach,
  Let me Thy Gospel riches teach.

Oh, Thou Wise and Holy God!
  Unfold the beauties of Thy Word,
Grant me that wisdom from above,
  To preach a dying Saviour's love.

To preach Salvation through the Cross,
  And count my sufferings here but dross;
To pray to Christ, the sinner's friend,
  To take me at my journey's end.

HYMN 234.

Love is the boon the Lord will give,
  To those who seek His gracious face;
Look unto Him, repent and live,
  And find with God a dwelling-place.

Love makes the heavenly arches ring
  With praises to the Son of God;
It makes the Saints and Angels sing,
  While millions spread His fame abroad.

Love moved our Maker's gracious breast
  To send the Prince of Glory down,
To guide us to His joy and rest,
  Before His face to wear a crown.

Love spreads the feast of Gospel Grace,
  That man may read and understand;
It guides us to our Saviour's face,
  And shows the path to His right hand.

HYMN 235.

Farewell, vain show and haughty pride!
  The soul of man needs something more;
Be Thou, oh, God! my help and guide;
  Direct me to that peaceful shore.

Show me the path Christ Jesus trod,
  His footsteps I would keep in sight;
The path most pleasing to my God
  Shall be my aim and chief delight.

Our Maker, God, is all in all;
  He guards our souls from day to day;
On His Almighty Name I call,
  To teach my sinful heart to pray.

HYMN 236.

" Come, learn of me !" the Saviour said ;
  "My yoke is easy, my burthen light;
And let thy heart on me be stayed;
  My great examples keep in sight.

" There be arrayed in blest attire,
  And all thy sins will be forgiven ;
In raptures tune that golden lyre,
  In my abode in yonder Heaven.

" This blessed day, come, hear my call !
  To-morrow's sun may seal thy doom ;
Here rests thy great Eternal All,
  Thine only hope beyond the tomb.

" My counsel unto man I give,
  To Adam's race while here below ;
Look up in faith, thy soul shall live,
  When free from Earth to glory go."

HYMN 237.

Why dost thine anger move so slow,
  When man profanes Thy holy name ;

Thine arm forbear to strike the blow ?
  To-day as yesterday the same.

Oh, God ! Thy power is over all,
  The high, the haughty, or profane ;
Saying, " Unto you, oh man ! I call !
  Why will ye take my name in vain ?

" I often called, but ye refused,
  With arms extended to receive,
Like that race, the wicked Jews,
  Ye seem unwilling to believe."

" But, oh repent !" God says, " Repent !
  Partake while there is room ;
Believe on whom the Father sent ;
  He calls on you to come !"

HYMN 238.

Oh, what a glorious theme is this,
  To sing our Maker's praise,
And walk the path of joy and bliss,
  To think upon our ways.

And while I walk life's rugged road,
   And Satan's malice feel,
I 'll bend my course for God's abode,
   With strong and fervent zeal.

Eternal Wisdom ! guide me on
   To that celestial shore ;
Grant me Thy grace to lean upon,
   Henceforth and evermore.

Lord ! can it be Thy holy will
   That I should see Thy face,
To sit and sing on Zion's Hill,
   And feast upon Thy grace ?

HYMN 239.

When man had sinned and fell from grace,
   And all was lost in dark despair,
The Saviour showed His gracious face,
   And offered His protecting care.

He died, the Heavenly Lover dies,
   The dreadful debt to pay ;

He made that woful sacrifice,
  With blood He marked the way.

From Heaven He brought salvation down,
  Our sin and guilt He bore ;
He offers man a richer crown
  Than ever monarchs wore.

The Jews blasphemed and still denied
  A Saviour being born ;
The Son of God they crucified,
  With mockery and scorn.

HYMN 240.

Thus while with awful sense I view
  Those slippery paths my feet have trod,
I fain would bid my sins adieu,
  And cleave to Him, the living God.

And worship Christ, the great Messiah,
  Who was, and is, and is to come ;
Give me that boon, a firm desire,
  And guide this weary pilgrim home.

Lord! guide us here from dark despair,
  And show how sin destroys our peace,
With kind compassion, love and care,
  And bid the tempter's rage to cease.

Direct us on life's rugged road,
  And wipe away each bitter tear;
Show us the path to thine abode,
  And softly whisper Thou art near.

HYMN 241.

May I from sin, oh God! depart!
  And cleave to Christ while there is room!
Lord, purify my sinful heart,
  By meek repentance may I come.

By true repentance, faith and love,
  May all my nobler powers agree
To try to meet Thee far above,
  And there the God of Jacob see.

There see that bright celestial throng,
And dwell where pleasures never die,
And sing that sweet Mosaic song,
With Saints and Angels far on high.

There see those massive gates of gold,
The songs of Zion sweetly sing,
Such joys by man cannot be told,
As makes God's high dominion ring.

HYMN 242.

Oh, Jesus, my Saviour! on whom I depend,
Oh, help us to praise Thee till life has an end;
Be pleased then to take us to glory above,
To sing Hallelujah in raptures of love.

To the rejoins of joy pray let me ascend,
To see my Redeemer, my Saviour, and friend;
The God of Compassion and Angels of light,
Where the day-star has risen and never comes night.

Ah, why should I wander, a stranger to God,
When my pardon was purchased by Jesus's blood?
The Prince of Salvation, who died to retrieve
The loss we sustained by the Devil and Eve.

In the midst of His anguish, when nailed to the tree,
In that dread gloomy Garden of Gethsemane,
He prayed to His Father, in anguish and love,
To view us in mercy and take us above.

The death of a Saviour was published around,
In the land of Judea where sin did abound,
The news of the Gospel was carried afar,
And thousands believed on the Bethlehem star.

The Scriptures were given in wisdom and truth,
To guide us to glory, both aged and youth

But if we neglect them and turn a deaf ear,
Despair is our portion I awfully fear.

HYMN 243.

There is a God in yonder skies,
Who is infinite in power;
A being Holy, just and wise,
Who guards us every hour.

A God of wisdom, love and grace,
Who orders all things right;
The wise will see His Sacred face,
For such are His delight.

In the third Heavens is His abode,
That Holy land of peace;
Oh, could we climb that Heavenly road,
And dwell where sorrows cease.

There see the city of our King,
And those who have gone before:
There songs and anthems sit and sing,
Henceforth and evermore.

HYMN 244.

The Son of God from glory came,
  And tasted death for sinners here;
He glorified His Father's name,
  While in the flesh He did appear.

He by the wicked Jews was slain,
  The Gospel pillars there He laid;
While on the Cross in Gethsemane,
  For sinners here He kindly prayed.

"Father, forgive them!" there He prayed,
  When they nailed Him to the wood;
"Let them repent, oh God!" he said;
  Yet they a-mocking round Him stood.

Psalms, or Spiritual Songs.

PSALM 1.

Blessed is the man who daily tries
To know and do His Master's will;
From sin's enchanting charms he flies,
And bends his course for Zion's hill.

He bends his course to Heaven above,
And holds communion with the Lord;
There views his Saviour dressed in love,
And reads and minds His Sacred word.

Blessed is the man who guards His feet,
And tries to walk the ways of truth;
He views and dreads the scoffer's seat,
And warns with care those giddy youths.

He fears to offend that righteous God,
And tries to keep His great commands;

He travels the path the Saints have trod,
   And views by faith that Holy land.

Grace, love and mercy have prepared
   A place of rest for all the Saints;
The humble and contrite will be spared,
   For God will hear their sad complaints.

Blessed is the man who fears to swear,
   Or take God's Sacred name in vain;
He guards his tongue and, lips with care,
   His viler passions doth restrain.

PSALM 2.

Blessed is the man who dares to say
   Christ is the true, the living way,
And daily reads His Holy Word,
   And trusts in his ascended Lord.

Blessed is the man who boldly stands,
   And views by faith the promised land,
And owns to all Christ's dying love,
   His thoughts aspire to Heaven above,

PSALM 3.

Blest is the man who shuns the place
Of sin and foul deceit,
And pleads the riches of His grace,
And bows at Jesus's feet.

Happy the man who fears to take
God's holy name in vain;
And tries while here his peace to make,
Eternal life to gain.

PSALM 4.

PSALMS — 119th CHAP.: 71st VERSE.

It is good for me that I have been afflicted.

The cup of affliction we fain would pass by,
From sickness and sorrow we wish to be clear;
Yet God has appointed we mortals must die,
Before His tribunal we all must appear.

In the midst of affliction, when sorrow and pain
Sweep like a deluge o'er body and mind:
Then trust in the Saviour, He will ever sustain,
He is full of compassion, both loving and kind.

The hand of affliction will soften the mind,
Teach us God's statutes, His precepts, His laws;
It shows us our Maker is loving and kind,
He never will chasten without any cause.

Help us in affliction to own and to bless,
And to cry—Abba, Father, the power is Thine;
Our sins and transgressions before Thee confess,
Our heart and our will to strictly resign.

PSALM 5.

Blessed is the man who shuns the road,
  That leads to sin and dark despair;
He searches to find the way to God,
  To place his heart, his treasure there.

Happy the man of Adam's race,
  Who holds communion with the Lord:
Who bows before His Throne of grace,
  And studies the riches of His word.

Blest is the man who tries to keep
  A conscience void of all offence;
Such as he sows he is sure to reap,
  With joy he meets his recompense.

Blest is the man who sees and knows,
  Who fears to walk the sinner's ways;
He grows in grace while on he goes
  To scenes of joy and brighter days.

PSALM 6.

PSALMS 31, VERSE 3.

Thou art my Rock: the Psalmist said,
The God I build my faith upon;
Oh, feed my soul with living bread,
Help me to gird my armor on.

Help me while in this vale of tears,
To gird my loins about with truth;
If I should live my three score years,
May I leave warnings to the youth.

PSALM 7.

Blest is the man who reads Thy word,
And trys to profit by the same;
With faith and love to serve the Lord,
In songs of praise to own His name.

The law of God is his delight,
He meditates both night and day;
God's holy cause he keeps in sight,
It helps to speed him on his way.

PSALM 8.

Why do the heathen rage and say,
  Their image is the living God;
Before their statutes kneel and pray,
  Deny the truth, God's Holy word.

Lord, send Thy heralds far and wide,
  And teach the heathen how to pray;
To those who have the truth denied,
  Convince them all Christ is the way.

PSALM 9.

Why do we mourn, lament and weep,
  When friends so dear from us are riven,
And hushed in death's cold, icy sleep?
  Their souls have tracked their way to
    Heaven.

Why do we mourn, in tears complain,
  Or shrink at death's cold, icy arm?

That dreadful cup, Christ drank the same,
To save our souls from sin and harm.

Why do we weep, or thus repine
For those who have gone to scenes of joy?
Ah! yes, to Heaven so pure, divine,
No sorrows can their peace destroy.

That Heaven, through faith, I hope to see,
In joy supreme beyond the skies;
For friends, why should we mourners be,
That dwell where glory never dies?

PSALM 10.

Christ, the Head, the Corner-Stone,
Our Advocate, our Grand High Priest;
The Great Messiah, the Holy One,
That spread for man the Gospel feast.

Christ is my refuge and my hope,
The Rock I build my faith upon:

Who bears my sinking spirits up,
  And bids me gird my armor on.

He pleads our cause with God above,
  To spare us in the world to come;
He kindly calls in words of love,
  And guides the ransomed sinner home.

Thou Rock of Ages, King of Saints,
  Who bore the Cross that we might live:
Oh, hear our cry, our sad complaints,
  And pardon all--oh, God! forgive.

PSALM 11.

Remember, Lord, my mortal frame,
  Grant me a hope beyond the grave;
May I adore Thy Holy name,
  Thine is the power, the arm to save.

Teach me Thy laws, to watch and pray,
  Then when I shall from earth remove,
When death shall steal my life away,
  I ask a place with Thee above.

When Christ shall in the clouds appear
  To judge the world, both quick and dead,
Oh, God! dispel my trembling fear,
  And feed my soul with living bread.

Since Christ in anguish died for me,
  I cannot slight or set at naught;
He has paid the debt, the penalty,
  The soul of man has dearly bought.

He ransomed all for Heaven above,
  Where myriads shout before His face,
And sing free grace, redeeming love,
  In God's abode or dwelling-place.

PSALM 12. Cor. 115c, 15v.

Christ died for all: the Scripture saith,
  All may repent and turn to God;
Give Him their heart and pray in faith
  For grace, through Christ's atoning
    blood.

Christ died for all that will repent,
The race of man He did retrieve;
He was, by God, the Father, sent,
That He, through mercy, could relieve.

Christ died for all the human race,
The Jew, the Gentile and the Greek;
His love to man and saving grace,
His death and sufferings loudly speak.

How can we slight or set at naught,
When Christ would claim us for His
own?
Our souls from sin with anguish bought,
And paid the ransom there alone.

He left the Heavens, His Father's throne,
The soul of man lay near his heart:
Came down and made salvation known,
The bread of life He did impart.

www.ingramcontent.com/pod-product-compliance
Lightning Source LLC
LaVergne TN
LVHW020233110826
845151LV00003B/910

* 9 7 8 1 4 2 5 5 3 1 1 7 1 *